Teen Fathers Today

TEEN FATHERS TODAY

TED GOTTFRIED

Twenty-First Century Books
Brookfield, Connecticut

In loving memory
of young adult book writer
Janet Bode

My gratitude to the late Janet Bode for her guidance and support in researching and writing this book. I would also like to thank those teen fathers in New York City, Hewlett, New York, and Tucson, Arizona, who agreed to be interviewed by me. I am also indebted to the personnel of the New York Central Research Library, the Mid-Manhattan Library, the Epiphany Branch Library, and the central branch of the Queensboro Public Library for their aid in researching material.

Their help was invaluable, but any shortcomings in the work are mine alone.

Ted Gottfried

Published by Twenty-First Century Books
A Division of The Millbrook Press, Inc.
2 Old New Milford Road
Brookfield, Connecticut 06804
www.millbrookpress.com

Library of Congress Cataloging-in-Publication Data
Gottfried, Ted.
Teen fathers today / by Ted Gottfried.
p. cm.
Includes bibliographical references and index.
ISBN 0-7613-1901-8 (lib. bdg.)
1. Teenage fathers—United States—Juvenile literature. [1. Teenage fathers.]
I. Title
HQ756.7.G68 2001
306.874'2—dc21   00-047931

Photographs courtesy of SuperStock: p. 3 (© Jamie Marcial); © Helen M. Stummer: pp. 8, 39, 55; Photo Edit: pp. 15 (© Tony Freeman), 18 (© Will Hart), 30 (© Spencer Grant), 48 (© Bonnie Kamin), 65 (© Cleve Bryant), 72 (© David Young-Wolff), 82 (© Merritt Vincent); © 1999 SHIA Photo/Impact Visuals: pp. 28, 79, 92; © Joshua Lermon: pp. 34, 37, 46, 102; SuperStock: p. 58 (© Scott Barrow), 100 (© Jin Jiang)

Contents

Teen Fathers Today

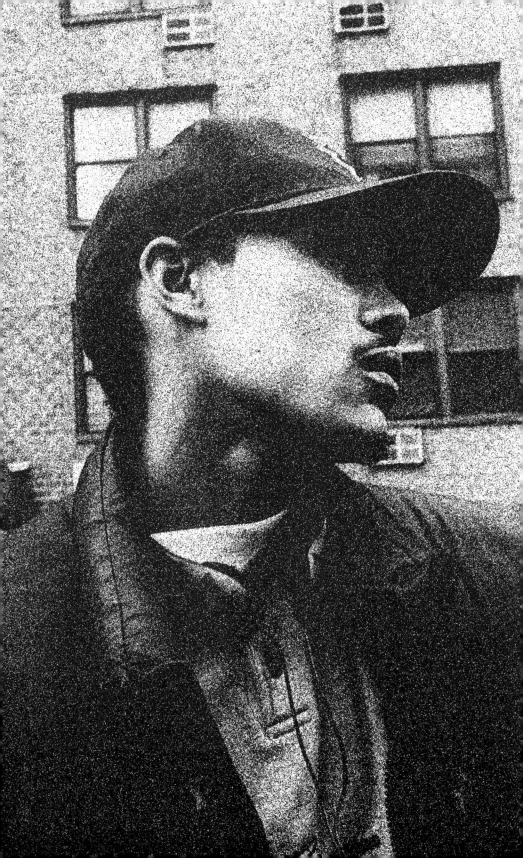

1.
THE MYTH AND THE REALITY

"My girl, Anita, got pregnant. I didn't mean for it to happen. First thing I know, it's all over the block. People, they look at me different. Guys kid me, I'm a stud. Older people, they think I'm no good 'cause my girl Anita, she's a nice girl. Thing is, nobody knows what I am, how I feel—inside, you know? They think they know, but they don't know, not really."[1]

—Cesar, 16-year-old father-to-be

Cesar is confused. Last month his biggest concern was passing geometry. This month he has to deal with his frightened girlfriend, with her parents, with his parents, with discussions of abortion, marriage, adoption—all kinds of things he never gave a thought to before. His whole future is unrolling before his eyes and, truthfully, he doesn't like what he sees. It scares him. It panics him. Does he love Anita? Does she love him? How does he feel about the baby? Does he even like babies? He never thought about that before. Sure, he's concerned about Anita, and, yes, the baby too. But what about himself? What's this going to do to his life?

Good News, Bad News

Every baby that is born has a father as well as a mother. As obvious as that seems, when it comes to teen parents—particularly unmarried teen parents—the father often gets lost in the shuffle. The focus is on the infant, as it should be, and on the mother who has gone through the trauma of childbirth and now faces the sometimes overwhelming responsibilities of motherhood. Nevertheless, the young father also has feelings and worries and responsibilities to face. He too may feel overwhelmed and alone, but actually he is one of many adolescent males who find themselves in this situation.

Although the National Center for Health Statistics reports that in 1998 teenage pregnancies in the United States fell for the seventh straight year "to a near-record low," they "still far exceed those in other industrialized countries." One study estimates that adolescent males share responsibility for 300,000 or more pregnancies in this country every year and that one out of every ten to twenty teenage males is involved in a pregnancy outside of marriage. Disturbing as these figures are, they don't begin to capture the practical and emotional impact of teen fatherhood.[2]

In recent years there has been a major shift in society's attitude toward unmarried teen mothers from condemning them to offering them sympathy and support. This may not always be true in individual cases, but for the most part the lot of the teen mother has improved. She usually gets more understanding than in the past.

This is not so true for the teen father. There are many misconceptions about him and his role, for instance:

How Casual Is Teen Sex?

Myth: Adolescent pregnancy is the result of casual sex. Boys who make girls pregnant are like bumblebees pollinating flowers. They move from girl to girl, having sex one or two times, and then they're on their way. They do not commit. They do not know the meaning of commitment. What they want is the instant gratification of sex. What they don't want is a long-term relationship.

Reality: Adolescent males may have strong sex drives, but they have other needs as well. They need to connect emotionally; they need to know that someone cares about them; they need security. It's a rare guy whose sex drive exists in a vacuum. Surveys show that one-night stands are the exception, not the rule.

A 1996 study in *Families in Society,* reported that "the majority of unwed teenage fathers had a relationship with the mother of the child for at least one year prior to pregnancy." In a survey of 170 teen mothers, the majority reported a "committed" relationship prior to conception. Other surveys bear this out.[3]

The Age Factor

Myth: Adolescent girls are usually made pregnant by older men. The male fantasy perpetrated by television and the movies is that mature men are much more attractive to young women than males their own age. Older men dominate because the father image is irresistible to immature females who require guidance in beginning their sex lives.

Reality: Many—perhaps most—adolescent females are uncomfortable with older men. They have more in common with boys their own age. They may be more at ease in sexual situations with someone as relatively inexperienced as themselves. Bearing this out, one survey of urban teen mothers found that 86 percent of their sex partners and 56 percent of their children's fathers were in their teens. Another survey reported 60.4 percent of the fathers of babies born to teen women were under the age of twenty.

Of course some adolescent women may be persuaded to have sex with older men. But then some young boys may also be persuaded to have sex with older women. In San Pedro, California, a woman in her twenties had a three-year affair with an eleven-year-old boy. He was under fourteen when she had a child by him. He is now fifteen, and she has been legally barred from any further contact with him, or any unsupervised contact with their child. His relationship with the year-old infant has yet to be determined.[4]

"Super Studs"

Myth: Teen fathers are "super studs" who are more knowledgeable about sex than the average adolescent male. Their macho image often requires that they have unprotected sex. The sex act for them is all ego and there is little feeling for the female involved.

Reality: Teen fathers don't usually know much about sex. They may be ignorant about the female body, and even about their own. Their ideas about how reproduction works may be muddled. One survey found that 56 percent of teen fathers had been educated about sex by a friend—usually one little older than themselves.

"When I told Jojo I was pregnant by him, he like went to pieces. He cried." Llona, age sixteen, shakes her head and finishes warming the bottle for six-month-old Danielle. "I felt so guilty. See, I didn't let him use a condom because it felt—you know—not really like love. He thought like I knew when I could and when I couldn't. Get pregnant, I mean. He was so innocent."[5]

In the past, Jojo's situation was not unusual. Many boys didn't use condoms because their sexual partners objected. "Over half the boys in one study said their girlfriends resisted using contraceptives."[6] Today, according to U.S. government demographer Stephanie J. Ventura, that has changed. She reports that today there is "more consistent use of birth control, especially condoms," among adolescents who are sexually active.[7]

Low Self-Image

Myth: Very different from the "super stud" theory is the idea that teen fatherhood is the result of low self-esteem. Adolescent males who have a poor image of themselves, or who have doubts about their masculinity, deliberately get a girl pregnant as a way of proving that they are men. They may deliberately neglect to use birth control to achieve this end.

Reality: While there may be some young males out there who pursue this course, there is no data to suggest that such behavior is commonplace. There may be subconscious reasons for choosing early fatherhood, but most teen pregnancies are accidental. Nevertheless, it is true that becoming a father may improve a young male's self-image.

"Before my child was born, I didn't think much of myself," says Arthur, who was sixteen years old when he became a father. Arthur lives with his parents in a Long Island suburb on a tree-shaded street in a restored Dutch colonial house with an in-ground swimming pool. His father is a lawyer; his mother a college instructor. "My father and mother are both successful. I'm their only child and I always had this feeling that I was falling short. I got mediocre marks in school and I wasn't much of an athlete and I guess I was sort of an introvert with people. Then I met Marcy, and she got pregnant and David was born. It all happened like that—so fast—and there was a lot of flak from our folks, both hers and mine, but now there's David. I'm his father and he looks up at me, and when he smiles, I'm some-body. Maybe Marcy and I will get married, and maybe we won't. But David will always be my son. I'm his father. I'll always be important to him. That makes me feel important to myself."[8]

The Race Card

Myth: The 1998 report by the National Center for Health Statistics revealing that "birthrates for Hispanic and African-American teenagers [are] still considerably higher than those for whites," indicates an ethnic or racial promiscuity factor driving adolescent males from these groups to make babies. Such activity is part of their genetic makeup.[9]

Reality: This isn't true. Such views may be a carryover from the days when blacks and Latinos were viewed as more sexually potent than whites—as sex symbols to be both feared and desired. In fact, teen fatherhood rates among Appalachian whites are equivalent to those among African Americans and Latinos. The cause-and-effect relationship is with poverty, not race or ethnic background.

As Latinos and blacks have moved up in the economy, the rate of teen births has "dropped precipitously." For African-

American teens, it is "the lowest birthrate since 1960." Sheila Clark, public policy associate at the National Black Women's Health Project believes that "when you give people in general—and African Americans in particular—increased access to education and employment, you increase their quality of life and reduce the number of unintended pregnancies."[10]

What About the Middle Class?

Myth: Because there is a cause-and-effect relationship between poverty and teen fatherhood, middle class and suburban youths are not at risk. With more stable home environments, better educations, and the higher morality central to middle-class values, they do not "run wild" the way less fortunate boys do. Therefore, they are less sexually active than inner-city adolescent males.

Reality: An increasing number of male teens from relatively affluent families and "good" backgrounds are fathering children. Teenage sex occurs among all classes of society. Economic status has no bearing on the sex urge one way or the other. Middle-class boys must come to grips with the issues that result from fathering a child just as poor boys must.

The difference in social and economic status, however, does play a part once pregnancy is established. Upper and middle-class adolescents—the males responsible as well as the pregnant girls—are more likely to seek abortions than poorer young people in their position. There is a perception (perhaps unfair, perhaps untrue) that a child will affect their future more severely than on the future of less well off adolescents. If it is decided to have the baby, the teen dad will have more financial support available to him from his family. He can continue with his education; he can provide child support; his life may be disrupted, but he will not know the financial pressure, which can prove so devastating to poor young men in his position.

What the college-bound adolescent may encounter, that the poorer boy may not, is strong moral disapproval. He does not come from a culture where out-of-wedlock births are common and accepted. It may be an embarrassment to his parents and family. Making a "nice" girl pregnant may make him a pariah.

..., rel...
baby may ha...
payments direc...
without her real...

A Very Pow...

Myth: The n...
acknowledge pater...
adulthood before t...
tions, responsibilitie...
run.

Reality: Some y...
that feeling often cha...
and the reality of hol...
ferent things. More th...
a very powerful feelin...
child takes over.

Teen father MM ex...
in the delivery room and...
And he looked at me . . ...
best way you can say it, ...
looks at you and your b...
catching the Holy Ghost ...

Often the teen dad be...
a means of ensuring that ...
described, that he will alway...
his child. He may fear tha...
mother won't last, but he wa...
to his child.

However, establishing ...
problem. Most adolescent dad...
They don't know what their leg...
have quite the legal weight of...
fight for his right to parent his ...
fathers feel is well worth waging...

The Ph

Myth: T
his baby or
there, uninv
perfectly con
selves. He shi

Reality: M
their baby's mo
relationship th
emotionally inve

Sometimes t
Father and moth
may not last. On
with other people
to maintain a relati
have a say in the
child's life.

Deadbeat Da

Myth: Young u
tributing financially t
paternity in order not
When ordered to cont
skip payments, make p
altogether.

Reality: Although m
hold only part-time jobs,
payments. A May 1998
report indicates that "yo
than older fathers." The
which found that teen fathe
port they can provide their
vide support with a loss of

Often the support prov
The mother may be receiving
for Needy Families (TANF)
eral agency, and conceals th
baby's father in order not to h

2.
FACING PREGNANCY: FEELINGS AND OPTIONS

"I work with young fathers. . . . Just being told you're going to be a father produces anxiety. Inside you feel stress. Outside, though, you're, 'Hey, it's cool. Let's swing with it.'"[1]

—Bill Cannon, Young Fathers Counselor,
The Door, New York City

A very small percentage of teen pregnancies have been planned by both parties, but for the most part, the news that a girl is going to have a baby and he is the father comes as a shock to the adolescent male. Suddenly there is an avalanche of questions to be answered, options to be considered, problems to be solved. There may be embarrassment, and sometimes there is shame. There is a welter of emotions, difficult to sort out, hard to understand. Almost never is the young male prepared to deal with the news that he is about to become a father.

In most cases he won't be dealing with it alone, and that may be a mixed blessing. The first person he'll have to consult with—and one who may have an even stronger voice in making decisions than his—is the girl he made pregnant. The first decision they'll have to face is what to do about the pregnancy.

Is Abortion an Option?

That first decision may also be the hardest. Does she want to have the baby? Does he want her to have it? Should they consider an abortion?

Abortion, as an idea, may be either a right or a sin, depending on what a person believes. Abortion as an act to be considered is something else. It may be a physical invasion of the body and a blow to the emotions. Nor is it only an ordeal for the female who goes through it. It is also often traumatic for the teen male involved. It is his fatherhood that is being prevented. He may have strong feelings about that.

Nevertheless, there are reasons why an abortion might be considered. Parenthood can bring drastic changes to young lives. How old is the girl? How old is the boy? Are they really old enough to be responsible parents? Again, does she really want to have the baby? That's a key question. The male should be involved in the decision, but in a practical sense she is the one who will make it, and will have to live with it. Nor should he regard an abortion as a tragedy that will ruin her life.

Heather was fourteen years old when she had an abortion. She's twenty now, and says, "I have absolutely no regrets. Sometimes I think, wow, I would have a five-year-old! There's no way I could have done it."[2]

Parental Consent

The decision to end fatherhood by agreeing to an abortion is affected by religious beliefs, ethnic and racial backgrounds, and family convictions. The Roman Catholic Church, the Orthodox Jewish and fundamentalist Christian establishments, and most Muslim denominations oppose abortion. In most of the non-European world's cultures, abortion is not an acceptable option. In the United States, African Americans, Latinos and Asian Americans have lower abortion rates than Caucasians. A 1996 study in *The Journal of Contemporary Human Services* found that "African-American adolescent males who impregnate are much more likely than their European-American counterparts to encourage their sexual partners to avoid abortion and therefore are more likely to become fathers as a result of unplanned pregnancies."[3]

Perhaps the first question the boy and girl will ask is whether their parents have to know? Can't they just go for the abortion without telling anybody? Actually, if the girl is under eighteen, they can't in the majority of states in this country. Those states have either parental consent laws or parental notice laws. That means that before the pregnant girl can get an abortion, she must first tell her parents she intends to get one.

Depending on what negatives the girl has told him about her parents and how badly she thinks they will react to the news that she is pregnant, the boy may want to cooperate with her in making an end run around them. It is possible to make an appointment to see a local judge and request permission to have the abortion without informing the girl's parents.

However, the judge must be convinced that there is good reason—perhaps the danger of violence, or a history of abuse in the family—not to inform them.

The Poor Have Children

Parents and other family members related to both the pregnant girl and the boy responsible usually will have strong feelings about abortion. Their religious convictions may forbid it. Where this is not the case, their feelings about abortion may relate to their economic status. Better-off parents may urge abortion as a solution because of the effect a child might have on the young people's plans for college and other aspects of their future. In middle-class families, keeping the pregnancy secret may be a primary consideration. A quick, discreet abortion may be the solution of choice for those living in the kind of small towns or suburbs where scandal is to be avoided at all costs.

Statistically, teen pregnancy is more common among poorer people. Many of them are Catholics or fundamentalist Christians, and therefore opposed to abortion. Even those who are not religious may be inclined to prefer out-of-wedlock births to abortion. Teen pregnancy is certainly a major problem in the inner city and among the rural poor, but it is not quite the disgrace it may be among people who are better off. Tri-generation living is more common among the poor. It follows that the decision regarding abortion may well be in keeping with that old song: "The rich grow richer, and the poor have children."

Still, the middle class aren't really rich. They are just better off than the poor. They may have worked hard for their children, and now—if their religion doesn't forbid it—they see abortion as the only solution that will not wreck their son's life. The pregnant girl's family may feel the same way. Both sets of parents may view abortion as the best way out of an unfortunate situation.

If the young people go along with this, they may experience unexpected feelings in the aftermath of the procedure. The college-bound young man whose fatherhood has been aborted may have feelings of regret, even of guilt. He may require some counseling to come to terms with the decision. However, that may not always be the case. There may be young men who feel, like Heather, that they made the right decision, and are glad that their lives were not sidetracked by the burdens of parenthood.

The Adoption Option

What if the two teens don't want an abortion? What if they talk it over and decide they really care for each other and want their baby? Their decision may spark the first confrontation between the adolescent male and the potential grandparents of his child.

It should be his decision, but teenagers rarely have incomes independent of their parents. Where will the money come from to feed and clothe the child? The financial obligations of fatherhood may mean having to quit school, to give up career goals. Does fathering a child mean he must marry the baby's mother? Does he want that? Does she? What are the sacrifices, and how strong is the commitment to making them? These questions, particularly the ones having to do with money, will be more urgent for teens from poorer families than for their middle-class counterparts.

There will be cases in which both teens and their parents share a strong religious opposition to abortion. There may be agreement that the girl should have the baby. But what then? The same problems are still there.

Perhaps the baby should be given up for adoption. Assuming the teen mother is willing to do that, how does the teen father feel about it? How does he feel about having a child and never seeing it? Some teen males will feel okay with that. They will view it as an acceptable compromise between abortion and the burdens of fatherhood. It may be the most practical solution for everybody concerned—teen father, teen mother, and baby. Many adolescent males, however, will have strong feelings for the child they helped create and will want some connection with that child. Often parenthood can be as important to males as to females. Parting permanently with one's child is not a step to be taken lightly by either teen mothers or teen fathers.

Today, however, that parting need not be permanent. Recent trends in adoption, known as open adoption, encourage a continuing relationship between birth parents— the teen father as well as the teen mother—and the adopted child. They replace former adoption procedures, which forbid contact between child and birth parents, and which usually contained secrecy provisions designed to keep the child from learning the identity of its birth parents. Now contact is maintained between the birth parents and the adoptive parents and the child from the start. Visits are scheduled; photos are taken; letters are exchanged. Maintaining such contact is considered beneficial to the child. It is also good for the teen father to feel that he hasn't abandoned his child, but rather continues to be involved in his child's life. Some experts, however, dispute the benefits of open adoption.

When making arrangements for adoption, teen parents should be careful. Not all agencies play by the new rules. Some cling to noncontact and secrecy agreements. A teen father should be careful to be sure that when he gives up his child for adoption, he is not giving away his right to be its father.

Other People's Input

Early on, the teen male will learn that his girl's pregnancy involves many more people than the two who brought it about. He may have to confront reactions he never anticipated. Anger is often the unfortunate, but understandable, reaction of the parents of adolescents in pregnancy situations. Her mother and father, frustrated at a circumstance that they had been unable to prevent, may jump to the conclusion that their daughter was seduced, blame the boy, and direct their wrath toward him.

His parents, likewise frustrated, may be furious with their son for wrecking his future. He has accepted responsibility for the pregnancy, but they may raise doubts. How does he know he's really the father? Maybe the girl was having sex with other boys. How can he be sure? He shouldn't let himself be trapped.

The suggestion makes him angry. He quarrels with his parents. His girl wouldn't do that. She's not like that. But they are his parents and soon there are nagging doubts.

Before long other relatives from both families become involved in the decisions that have to be made. Grandparents, uncles and aunts, siblings—it seems everybody has an opinion, and feels entitled to take a moral stance. His girl is being buffeted from all sides just as he is. They try to cling together in the face of mounting disruption, but are soon passing along family members' opinions to each other and often disagreeing about them.

Confused, not sure what he wants to do, or what he should do, the boy may turn to his male friends for advice. If he's lucky, one or two of them will be truly sensitive to his situation. Some will treat it as a joke. He got caught. Luck of the draw. Others may be more interested in the sex he had than in the pregnancy. Still others will give him macho advice: Walk away from it; she wanted it, it's her lookout; that's how they trap guys, get themselves pregnant. It's a rare friend his own age who will have the wisdom and life experience to help him deal with his confusion, his feelings, and his responsibilities.

Counseling, Help, and Support

There are people out there, however, who are ready, willing, and qualified to help the prospective teen father. He may get the help he needs to clarify his situation from a teacher, a guidance counselor, a school social worker, or a therapist. His minister, priest, or rabbi is available for counseling. If he has a family doctor, the doctor might be the one to help him. Sometimes just talking to an adult who is making the effort to understand rather than to judge him will be the greatest help of all.

Many communities have counseling and support groups for teen fathers-to-be. The Urban League offers a Teen Fathers/Male responsibility program in many cities. The National Institute for Responsible Fatherhood sponsors helpful programs like the Teen Father Program in Cleveland, Ohio. East St. Louis, Illinois, offers counseling at the Father's Center. The state of Tennessee has a Responsible Teen Parent Program, which offers counseling. AltaMed Youth Services in Commerce, California, provides case management services for expecting and/or parenting adolescents, both male and female between the ages of eleven and eighteen. In New York City, The Door offers programs and counseling for both prospective teen fathers and male teens who are already parents.

Some communities have branches of the Maximizing a Life Experience (MALE) program, which focuses on the three Rs: rights, responsibilities, and resources. MALE's goals are to help the young men express feelings and concerns, provide emotional support, help clarify their responsibilities, explain their legal rights, and give them information about available resources. Information about these and other programs is available from the Office of Educational Research and Improvement of the U.S. Department of Education. (See *Organizations to Contact,* p. 120.)

Paying for Pregnancy

Many of these organizations will support the teen male through the pregnancy, birth, and on into fatherhood. In the beginning, however, the pressure of time may act against his getting such help, or of it being effective if he does get it. During those first days with families pushing him and the pregnant girl one way and another, there will be a need to make decisions quickly, and perhaps without outside support.

In those cases where abortion and adoption are ruled out, he will be drawn into a supporting role toward the mother-to-be of his child. There are things about pregnancy that he probably never gave a second thought to before. For one thing, there are expenses. Her family may want him to share them. Doctor bills, drugs, birth classes, pregnancy clothes, baby clothes—these things cost money. If the pregnant girl had been helping to support her family with a part-time job and the time comes when she must stop working, this will put a financial burden on her family, which he may be expected to share. The poorer the father-to-be, the more pressure this will put on him.

This is not yet the burden of child support. That will come later. This is only the initial financial strain of impending fatherhood. Because it follows so quickly on the knowledge of pregnancy, it may come down on the adolescent male like a ton of bricks. "I'm still going to school, and I'm working every day unloading trucks," says Cesar, a 16-year-old father-to-be, "but I got no money to even take Anita to a movie account of her father says I have to pay my share or I can't see her."[4]

Dealing with Mood Swings

Supporting the mother-to-be of his child doesn't just mean providing money. It also means providing the kind of emotional support all pregnant women need. This may not always be a simple matter even for older, married males. When a person is going through pregnancy, the changes her body is undergoing are accompanied by emotional mood swings. This is normal. However, for the inexperienced teen father-to-be, relating to these mood swings and continuing to be supportive may sometimes be difficult and confusing.

Add to these mood swings the pressure of the young woman's situation—she's unmarried, there are financial pressures, her family may be disapproving and not supportive, they may constantly be bad-mouthing the teen father. Providing emotional backup to her in such circumstances may be no easy matter. As her body changes, she may feel unattractive. She may worry about the father-to-be's interest in other girls. She may berate him for the pregnancy when he comes around, and when he doesn't come around, she may feel neglected. She may cling to him and shower him with kisses one day and curse him out the next.

If he cares about her, and about his unborn child, he'll try to keep an even keel through all of this. He'll sympathize with her morning nausea, assure her that her pregnant body is more beautiful than ever, try to get along with her parents no matter how hostile they may be, reassure her that he'll stick by her through the birth of their child and beyond. He'll be her best friend through it all.

Preparing for Childbirth

Even if marriage is not being considered, even if they're not that committed to each other, he'll stick by her. That will be necessary if he wants to have a relationship with his child after he or she is born. Most teen fathers do. "Most teenage fathers care about what happens to their children," according to the Educational Resources Information Center (ERIC) Clearinghouse on Counseling and Personnel Services. They want an ongoing relationship with them.[5]

Toward that end, he should go through as much of the child-bearing experience with the girl as possible. If he wants to bond with his child he should think about being there during the birth. He may want to attend Lamaze classes, or other birth preparation classes, with the mother-to-be.

Lamaze is a method to prepare the mother for childbirth. She is taught relaxation techniques and special breathing and pushing exercises. The father-to-be, or another person, who chooses to be with her during the delivery is called a coach, and he (or she) also receives instruction. The purpose is to make the delivery as comfortable as possible for the mother. She will be fully conscious during the process and—except in special cir-cumstances—no drugs will be used. It is important that the

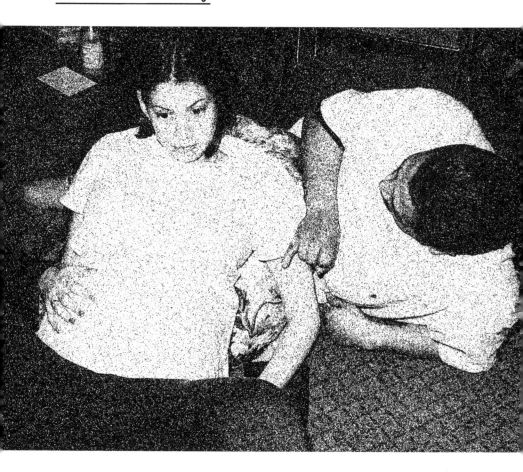

teen father-to-be understand what she will be going through, that there will be some pain, and what his role will be in alleviating it.

Teen father Ron describes what the classes are like: "The Lamaze teacher showed me how I should help Donna breathe through her nose, in a rhythm. She had us practice where I would rub Donna's weak spots, wash her face with a cool rag, gently touch and rub her back—always rub down, never up, she said. The teacher also said that I had to tell Donna to relax . . ."[6]

Some women don't want to use the Lamaze technique. They know giving birth can be a painful experience and they want to be given painkillers. This isn't a decision the teen father-to-be should argue about. It's her body, her pain, her choice.

Still, it isn't easy for him. These are probably things he's never thought about before. "Studies now show that most teenage fathers do not have it all together and are just as confused, afraid, and anxious as the young women they impregnate." To become a father can be a wonderful experience, but the prospect can be scary. There's so much to deal with, and the baby hasn't even been born yet.[7]

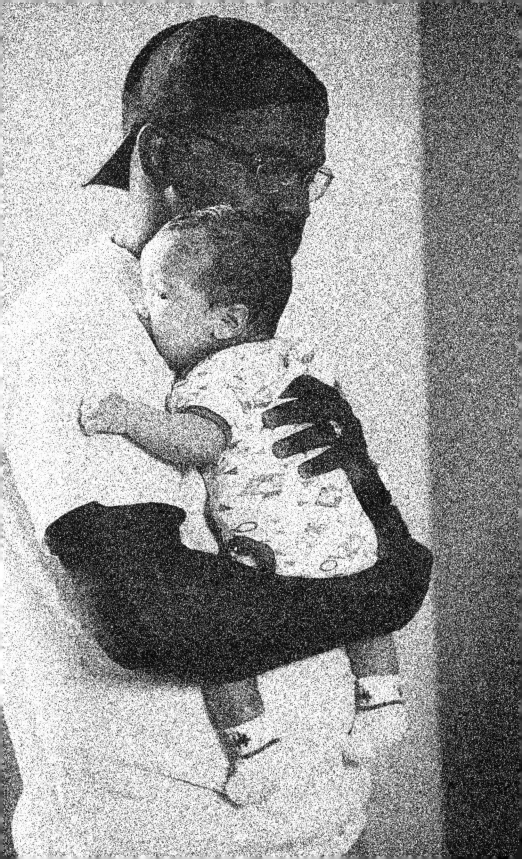

3.
BEING A DAD

"I just think a father should be in there, to go through the experience, you know, to see what the mother goes through. . . . . It's like you see your son or daughter come out and you're there and that's where everything starts. I think the most important thing is to be there for my daughter. I need to give her love and understanding. A father is the one who makes you smile. Being a father means being there for everything."[1]

—Teenage father F. Q.

_____

The birth of the child is also the birth of the teenage father. It is both a torrent of joy and an avalanche of responsibilities, some of them unforeseen. "Many young men are giving up on their families because they don't know how to be fathers," according to the Reverend Phoenix Barnes Jr., of the Fathers' Center in East St. Louis.[2]

Each day of teen fatherhood brings new problems. Much time can be wasted in just learning how to cope with them. It's as important for the new father to know what to expect as it is for him to learn what to do in order to bond with his child. Following are some situations illustrating what teenage fathers don't know—and what they should know—about child care and related matters:

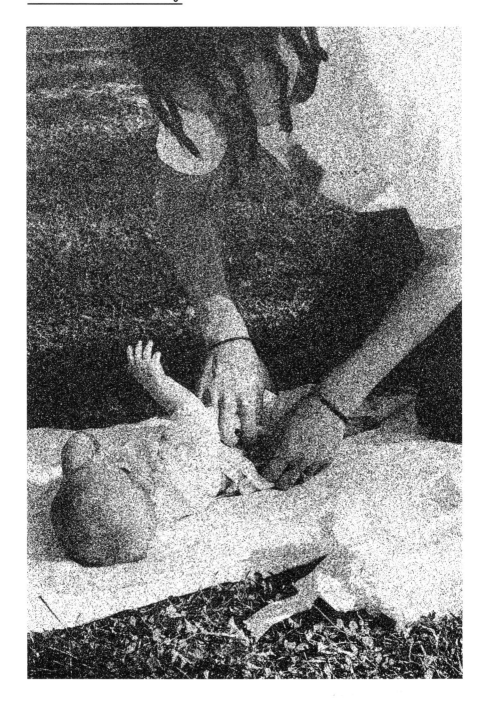

Whether using disposables, a service, or reusing cloth diapers, before diapering the baby, the teen father should know what he's doing. He should get someone with experience to show him how to change the diaper. He should learn how to position the baby while diapering it, how to clean and powder the infant, perhaps how to use safety pins with cloth diapers without sticking the baby, and how to dispose of used diapers. It's not really hard, but if the teen father is nervous, he should practice—perhaps with a doll—before diapering the baby.

"First time I diapered Ronald," remembers Alec, "I was like afraid to even pick him up. Laurie, she's bouncing him around like a bag of groceries, and I'm afraid I'm gonna break him. Now, though, I'm a real pro."[6]

Some experts believe that changing the baby's diaper is—along with feeding the baby—a primary opportunity for bonding with the child. The baby's love for the father may begin with easing the infant's discomfort. When crying turns into a gurgle, and that expression of discontent into the beginnings of a smile—that's the moment the teen father may feel most deeply that this child is his. "You're hooked," is the way Alec put it. "Your kid has hooked you and you stay hooked for good."[7]

Feeding Time

A teen father's first experience with feeding his child probably won't involve him directly at all. In most cases (but not all), the baby's mother will choose to breast-feed the infant. There will be a closeness involved, which can not include the father. Many fathers—not just teens—have an emotional reaction to this. They feel excluded. They may even feel jealous. Because this is common, even to be expected, it's important that the teen father understand why breast-feeding is important to his child.

The first reason is colostrum—"the fluid that comes in before the real milk." As early as the 1950s, Dr. Benjamin Spock, then the world's leading pediatrician, suggested that colostrum "might provide some protection against certain diseases." Since then, scientific research has confirmed that colostrum plays an important role in building up the immune system. Dr. Spock emphasized "the confidence and pleasure breast-feeding can provide for a mother and the sense that she is satisfying her child's basic emotional and nutritional needs." He also pointed out—and it is still true—that breast-feeding is less expensive than buying formula and bottles.[8]

Dr. Spock's views on breast-feeding are widely accepted today by experts like Dr. T. Berry Brazelton and Dr. Penelope Leach, Ph.D. However, modern experts also recognize that there are circumstances that call for compromises in breast-feeding. It's important for the teen father to be aware of these circumstances and to adjust to them as an early part of establishing a relationship with his child.

Breast milk is digested more quickly than formula, and so the breast-fed baby is apt to want to be fed often. This can be as frequent as every hour or two throughout the night. The teen mother's breasts may become sore, and she may become irritable from lack of sleep. When breast feeding is not a happy experience for her, the baby senses it and is also not happy.

In many cases, the ideal compromise is to alternate breast-feeding with formula feeding from a bottle. This allows the teen father to take over some of the feeding duties. To what extent will vary with individual cases. "It has to be your decision," is the advice that Dr. Leach gives to teen mothers. While Dr. Leach is sympathetic to the burden on teen fathers, she believes that only the mother can decide how much, or how little, breast-feeding is best for herself and her child. The teen father should be prepared to accept this without arguing about it. In cases where the teen mother goes out to work, breast-feeding may not be practical at all. Here the teen father should be ready to share the bottle feeding burden with the mother.[9]

Feeding: A Two-Way Street

When the teen father takes on feeding duties, both parents should already have decided whether the child will be fed on demand or according to a predetermined schedule. There are arguments for both courses. Some pediatricians feel that feeding the baby on demand—whenever he or she is hungry—

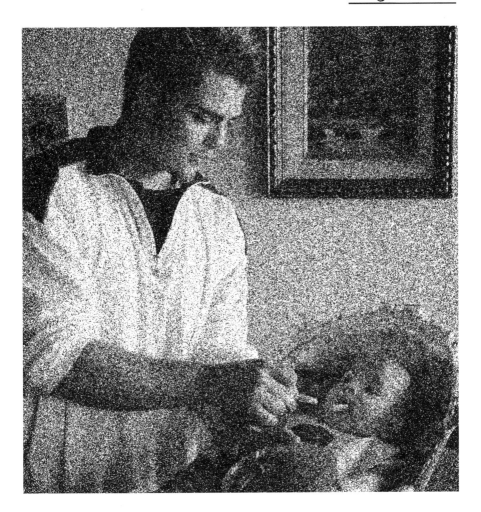

makes for a happier, more contented child. Others feel that
demand feeding may spoil the child, accustom it to the kind of
instant gratification that interferes with developing the patience
it will need in adulthood. They believe that easing the child into
a regular feeding schedule is a necessary part of the maturing
process. Another determining factor is the difficulties that both
courses may present for the teen parents. Is it easier for them to
react to the child's hunger spontaneously or to regiment themselves in keeping with the feeding schedule they have set up for

the baby? Dr. Spock concluded that it was not very important "whether a baby is fed purely according to his own demand" or on "a regular schedule." What was important, he concluded, was the flexibility to "adjust to the baby's needs and happiness." An infant should never be allowed to cry for lengthy periods if he or she is hungry.[10]

Before feeding his baby, there are things the teen father should know. For instance, before using new bottles, nipples, and rings, they should be sterilized by submerging them in a pot of boiling water for at least five minutes and then set to dry on a clean towel. Before feeding the baby, the bottle of formula should be warmed in a pan of hot—not boiling—water or by running it under the hot-water tap. A microwave should never be used; it can break down the nutrients in the formula. The right temperature is important. Too cold and the baby won't take it. Too hot and it could burn the baby. The teen father can test the temperature by releasing a drop on the back of his hand.

He'll have to recognize when the formula is flowing freely so that the baby doesn't have to suck in vain, and he'll have to judge when too much formula is going through the bottle nipple and making the baby gag, or choke. Noisy sucking sounds indicate that the baby is taking in too much air. Holding the infant at a 45-degree angle may relieve the problem. The bottle should be tilted so that the nipple and neck are always filled with formula. It should never be propped. That can cause the baby to choke.

Like diapering, feeding helps the teen father to bond with his baby. This is a two-way street. The infant is nurtured and she or he loves back. The father can't help but recognize that at this moment he is the most important person in his baby's life. That's a responsibility, but it's one that he's meeting, and that can be a big boost to his ego.

Bathing the Baby

Bathing a slippery, squirming, sometimes howling infant is not exactly a night out with the guys for the teen dad. Still, the more he does it, the easier it gets. The baby gets more comfort-

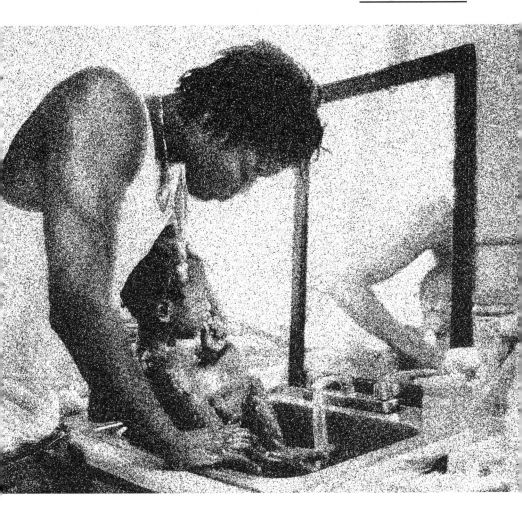

able with the bath too and begins to have fun splashing and playing in the water.

One of the questions teen fathers ask is how often the baby should be bathed. Really, it depends on the age of the child. Babies who haven't started to crawl yet don't get that dirty. Two to three baths a week are enough as long as the diaper area is kept clean and the hands and face are washed. As they get older, though, an every-night bath may be necessary. This has the added advantage of calming the toddler down at bedtime.

Up to six months, the best time to bathe the infant is before meals. After eating, the baby may spit up and have to be bathed all over again. A good idea is to work the bath into some regular routine including playtime, or reading a story, and bedtime.

In the very beginning—up to three weeks after birth—it's best to sponge bathe the baby so that the umbilical cord stump doesn't get wet. If a male baby is circumcised, as is still the custom in most hospitals, new parents should follow carefully the doctor's instructions on how to care for the affected area. The baby should be laid on a soft, flat surface such as a clean towel. Using warm water and a sponge, one limb at a time should be uncovered, washed, and patted dry. Only after the stump has fallen off, should the baby be given a regular bath.

This can be done in a baby tub or in an ordinary sink. The bottom should be padded with a towel. For safety's sake, not more than 2 inches (5 centimeters) of warm water should be used. If the room is even mildly chilly, a warm washcloth should cover the baby's tummy. Water alone is usually enough to clean the baby, but if soap is used, it should be baby soap. Ordinary soap removes natural moisturizers and the dry skin which results is uncomfortable for the baby. The infant should be held firmly, its head cradled, and any dirt or loose skin should be gently washed away. The teenage dad should pay special attention to the baby's genitals and backside, the areas between the fingers and toes, armpits, the folds of flesh at the back of the neck, knees, and elbows, and behind the ears. If there is gook in the area of the eyes, a damp cotton ball should be used to remove it. Baby shampoo can be used to clean hair and scalp, but care should be taken so that it is thoroughly rinsed off.

The baby should never—never!—be left alone during a bath. This goes for toddlers as well as infants. Dr. Alfred T. Lane of the Stanford University School of Medicine stresses that "babies can drown in as little as 1 inch (2.5 centimeters) of water—and in the time it takes to answer the doorbell or phone."[11]

Playtime

From the first, playing with a baby is important. It's key to establishing that bond between teen father and child, but it's also important to the development of the infant. Early play is observing, listening, and experiencing. It's how babies explore and learn about their world. Everything is new to babies, and although they have short attention spans, they are naturally curious and respond to sights and sounds and the taste, smell, and feel of things.

Playing begins with getting the baby's attention. At first he or she will focus on objects 8 to 10 inches (20 to 25 centimeters) away. As the infant gets older, that range will increase. The baby will identify seeing Daddy with the sound of his footsteps. When the teen dad plays with his baby, the infant will relate the pleasure of play with being with him.

At first this play will consist of using simple objects to attract the baby's attention. Basic toys—rattles, mobiles, music boxes, small flashlights, squeaky dolls, child-safe mirrors, cloth books, soft animals or balls, teething rings, anything that will stimulate the child's senses with patterns of light and dark and colors and images and unusual sounds and textures—are best for early play. The "sensory stimulation" such play provokes "literally 'lights up' areas of your baby's brain," says Dr. Kathleen Alfano, Ph.D., of the Fisher-Price Child Research project. That light shines on the teen father providing the stimulation. It is an important building block of the relationship between him and his child.[12]

As the baby gets older, the teen father should interact with him or her more. Playing peekaboo—hiding his face behind his hands and then revealing it—will usually delight the baby. It can go on forever until one day—suddenly—the baby loses interest in seeing Daddy's face pop out from behind his hands. It's time for a new game, but at first it still has to be kept simple. Showing the baby a stuffed animal and then hiding it behind the back may arouse the infant's curiosity. Showing the infant two or three stuffed dolls, hiding them, and then coming out with one or two will introduce the baby to the idea that something is missing. Puzzlement will give way to understanding, and soon the baby will recognize that something is being added or subtracted. In a way, the teen father is giving his child a first arithmetic lesson.

Toddler Toys and Games

All babies are different, but somewhere between the ages of a year and eighteen months, simple problem-solving toys should be introduced into the teen father's playtime with his child. These can provide more advanced interaction, but it's important to recognize that there's no "right way" to play with them. Whatever the child does with them is okay. The teen father shouldn't try to correct him or her.

Activity toys are usually inexpensive. Ones that work best at this age are large plastic snap-together beads, simple nesting toys, and toys with large dials and levers that perform simple tasks, stacking blocks and ring-cones, and pop-up toys and books. These are trial-and-error toys and playing with them educates the baby as to how things fit together and how they work. There will come a moment when the baby does something that he or she recognizes as an accomplishment and the delight that it brings is something the teen father will not want to miss sharing with his child.

Between the ages of one and two years, as the baby is becoming a toddler, all of the time the teen father spends with his child should be both playtime and a time of learning. Toddlers are curious. Many things are new to them. They are keen observers who take in more than they can understand. The teen father should patiently explain these new things to his child. He should clarify activities like cooking, vacuuming, inserting batteries in a toy, programs on television, and so forth. He should take the toddler to new places, provide him or her with new experiences such as movies, a visit to a zoo, or a kiddy park. Always, he should talk to the child so that he or she will have some understanding of what they are doing together.

This is the age at which picture books and pop-up books become important to a child's development. Teen parents who don't know what is appropriate should consult with the children's librarian at the local library. He or she will know about the latest books for children and may have suggestions that will be helpful. Most libraries have excellent collections of children's literature, and the books can be taken out for two or three weeks at no charge. Videos for children may also be available. However, the teen father should be aware that watching videos should be limited during the first few years to protect the child's developing eyes.

Reading inspires imagination, and imagination leads to make-believe. This is an important activity for teen fathers to share with their two-and-three-year-old toddlers. However, the child is the author and director of the make-believe activity and the teen father is only an actor. It's all right to gently prod the toddler when he hits a snag in the story, but he shouldn't try to rewrite the toddler's script. If the teen dad wants to play in his child's imaginary world, he has to play by his rules. That can be frustrating, but it can also be one of the joys of fatherhood.

Toilet Training

Many young fathers regard toilet training as the point at which their child emerges from babyhood into childhood. However, that's not actually the case. There is rarely a relationship between toilet training and development in other areas. Put another way, while toilet training is a stage, it's not necessarily related to such other stages of development as talking coherently, walking upright, manual dexterity, socializing, or exhibiting intelligence. Nor are comparisons between children of the same age valid when it comes to toilet training. Some are ready for the process earlier than others, some have greater control over urination and bowel movements, and some are trained faster.

According to Dr. Glenn P. Matney, "most children are ready for potty training at about two years of age, some by eighteen months, others not until two and a half years, and the girls usually beat the boys by at least a few months." By the age of three most children are in control of these functions during the day. However, Dr. Matney points out, "it is very common and normal for a child to take even several more years to be fully dry every night."[13]

Sharing in his child's life means that the teen father must be a part of its toilet training. His first task may be buying either a potty, or a special-sized seat to attach to the toilet. It should be structured so the child can push with his or her feet during bowel movements. There are many picture books for children that explain toilet training and it's a good idea to get one out of the library and go over it with the child.

A routine should be created to get the child used to the idea of toilet training. It can begin with the child sitting on the potty at the same time every day with his or her clothes on. This should be eased into, never forced, and postponed if the child seems afraid. If there's no trauma, after a while the child should be placed on the potty without a diaper. The teen father can explain that this is what grown-ups do. They undress before they go to the bathroom. When the child poops in its diaper, it should be emptied into the potty to demonstrate the connection with sitting on the potty. Sooner or later the child will start to use the potty, but the teen father should never push it, and should never show impatience. After the child goes on the potty, he or she should be encouraged to wash their hands and put their clothes back on the way big people do.

It should be made clear to children that they can use the potty by themselves whenever they feel the need. However, some children are at first afraid to use the potty by themselves. Daddy should make sure they know they can ask him to take them to the bathroom. All children have setbacks and the teen father should be patient with this. He should never get angry, or punish the child for not making it to the potty. The trick is to stay calm, clean up the mess, and remind the child that he should maybe not wait so long to get to the potty next time. Potty training should never be treated as discipline.

Discipline

According to a 1997 survey by *Family Planning Perspectives,* "Young fathers expected to have half or more of the responsibility for disciplining their child . . . but less than half or none of the responsibility for changing diapers and for bathing the child." As we have seen, dodging those responsibilities means losing the chance to bond with one's child. More importantly, the teen father who establishes himself as a disciplinarian rather than a committed parent may end up seeming more like a jailer to his child than a dad.[14]

The first thing he should know is that there's a difference between discipline and punishment. Physical punishment is a flat-out no-no. Studies show that teen parents are more likely to be child batterers than older parents. Patience is a mark of maturity, and maturity is what a teen father must have no matter how old he is. Striking a child is neither discipline nor punishment, it's the act of a bully picking on someone too small to strike back.

Hitting only teaches the child to hit. It's okay to discipline the child with words, but both yelling and sarcasm should be avoided. Calmness is the best fatherhood tool a teen can have. The adolescent dad should always consider the state of the child—is he or she overtired? hungry? upset? stressed?—and his own state as well. It's not a good idea to discipline a child when one's patience is wearing thin. A better idea is to take a time-out.

The teen father should remember that most children want to please their parents and to do what they want them to do. Sometimes the best solution to a child's misbehaving is simply to direct its attention to something else. Communication is also important. When a parent is displeased with a child, it's important to be very specific about just what he wants the child to do. Simply telling him or her to behave can be misunderstood, or be reacted to as a challenge for more mischief. "Stop blowing that horn," "Pick up your toys," or "Put on your pajamas" are the kind of exact commands that are more likely to get results.

Parents should try to hold down the number of noes they put on their child. The adolescent dad should limit himself to those that are really important to the child's safety and well-being. Trying to impose his will when it comes to matters like food or clothes will rarely be effective. It's not a good idea to establish a hostile atmosphere between father and child, and too many rules can do that.

Of course, some discipline is necessary. It's a matter of sticking to those issues that are truly important. Keeping one's cool should always be the rule. Fairness and evenhandedness count. In the end, the child will recognize that the discipline is for his or her own good if it is fair—even if the child doesn't always admit it.

There's not usually much in his education that has prepared the young male for such problems of fatherhood as discipline, toilet training, diapering, and bathing and feeding his baby. As teen father G. K. put it, "I didn't think there was this much responsibilities. I mean, there's hundreds of 'em. Some weeks I plan for me and my child to do somethin' the whole week and it's like, and I didn't know in between he was going to wet his clothes, and now I gotta change him, and I gotta do this, and I gotta do that." Yes, it can all be pretty overwhelming, but many teen fathers have found that it really can be worth it.[15]

4.
THE MONEY DILEMMA

"We're not all deadbeat dads. Some of us are trying hard to do what's right."[1]
—Zachary, eighteen-year-old teen father

Doing right by his child financially involves more for the adolescent father than just being willing to face up to his responsibilities. He must also be able to provide the money necessary to support his child. However, still in his teens himself, the problem is that he lacks the education, training, and experience to earn enough to meet his child's needs.

The Children's Defense Fund reports that in 1997 (the latest year for which figures are available) "the unemployment rate for teenagers was three times as high" as for other workers and that "the economic return for their labor has diminished." In other words, there are fewer jobs available for young fathers, and those that are available pay less than in previous years.[2]

The teen dad's situation is made worse by the confusion and restrictions surrounding the various aid programs which are supposed to help young parents who can't make it financially on their own. The way the systems—federal, state, and local—are set up, it is a full-time job keeping up with their intricacies and frequent changes. In addition, most youngsters who are parents are unaware of their rights and of many of the benefits available to them. Lack of know-how in dealing with a welfare system that is constantly reorganizing is a common dilemma for all its clients, including teens.

The Dependency Cycle

Today the government aid programs available to teen parents are shaped at state and local levels. They may vary greatly from one place to the next, but all of them receive much of their funding from the federal government.

Federal involvement goes back to 1935 when Congress passed the Social Security Act and President Franklin D. Roosevelt signed it into law. One of the programs set up under that law was Aid to Families with Dependent Children (AFDC). It was designed to give assistance to children in one-parent homes. In 1935 when the program started, 88 percent of those who received aid were widows with dependent children. By the 1990s more than 50 percent of the recipients were unwed mothers and their children. Many of the mothers were teenagers.

As welfare costs mounted throughout the 1980s and 1990s, AFDC assistance began increasingly to be viewed as contributing to a welfare cycle in which poor women—often teens—had babies who grew up to themselves become teen fathers and mothers. Instead of helping, it was charged, AFDC was making dependency a lifestyle. As drugs became more and more of a problem among young people in poor neighborhoods, the perception grew that AFDC aid funds were being used to buy crack and other drugs rather than to help children. There was no hard evidence that this was happening to any great extent, but there was plenty of reason to believe that the welfare system—and AFDC in particular—was not working the way it was supposed to work. From all sides of the political arena there came demands that a way must be found to break the dependency cycle.

Temporary Assistance
for Needy Families

Reform came with The Personal Responsibility and Work Opportunity Reconciliation Act signed into law by President Clinton on August 22, 1996. It was a welfare plan requiring work in exchange for assistance. It did away with AFDC and replaced it with a program called Temporary Assistance for Needy Families (TANF). Under TANF, the states receive block grants of federal funds and are granted wide flexibility to develop and implement their own aid programs. Some states divide up the money and allow communities to shape the programs. Others retain control and set up standards and rules for the programs that apply in different areas and cities.

One purpose of the new law was to consolidate several programs into one. The goal was to relieve the burden of dealing with several bureaucracies on those applying for aid. Unfortunately, because of the ways in which state and local governments have set up their programs, this goal is far from having been met. Financial aid, food stamps, health care vouchers, job training programs, and a variety of other agencies may still have to be dealt with separately by teen parents in need. Much of the way the teen father will function financially in his new role will be determined by where he lives.

Certain federal rules, however, remain in effect for all areas of the country. TANF requires unmarried parents—teen fathers as well as mothers—to stay in school and live at home. This rule has turned out to be hard to enforce. Many teen males were school dropouts before they became fathers. Many from poor backgrounds had to give up school in order to work. Some families have refused to take on the responsibility of a teen pregnancy and the adolescent parents have had to make other living arrangements. Also, the law requires that the teen father work in exchange for short-term assistance and that he contribute to the support of his child. But working, going to school, sharing household tasks, and child rearing may simply prove too much of a burden for him. The burden is increased by the difficulties of following the paper trail through the welfare bureaucracy.

"Like I couldn't believe it after Danielle was born, all the places we had to go, just to get started," says seventeen-year-old Jojo of New York City. "First thing Llona says is we don't get married because the TANF help money is for single mothers. I'm still not clear that's right. Anyway, she gets some rent money and some food stamps and some clinic vouchers for the baby. But it's all like temporary, you know. And all the time the governor, the mayor, the feds, they're changing the rules. They say there's job training for teen fathers, but that means giving up my bike messenger job, which is off the books, and then we'd have less money. You want to do the right thing, but no way they let you know what that is."[3]

Deadbeat Dads

Jojo is correct. "The right thing" to do is hard to pin down. For instance, the federal government says that young mothers receiving money under the TANF program must assign their child support rights to the government. If Jojo complies with the law and makes support payments to Llona for Danielle, the law says she can keep no more than fifty dollars a month of that money. The rest goes to the government to pay back TANF payments and payments from other programs.

Like many other young fathers, Jojo doesn't make official child support payments. Instead, he gives Llona money for Danielle under the table. Statistically, he's a deadbeat dad, one of many unmarried fathers who deliberately avoid supporting their children. Actually, Jojo is demonstrating concern and love for his child. He is making sure the money is used for Danielle, rather than having it taken by the government.

Jojo is one of those teen fathers who quit school in order to earn enough money to at least partially support his child. He fears that like many others in his situation, this decision will result in his being trapped by lack of education in low-paying jobs, which won't provide enough income to meet Danielle's increasing expenses as she grows older.

Many teen fathers trapped in this fashion feel inadequate and become severely depressed. They are ashamed of not being able to support their child and their self-image suffers. Sometimes they feel they have let down their child. They can face neither the child, the teen mother, nor the situation. It's all too much for them. According to a 1995 study published in *Marriage & Family Review*, "many disadvantaged fathers feel inadequate about their ability to fulfill the breadwinner role and often dissociate themselves from it in order to minimize their sense of inadequacy." Shame drives them away, and they relinquish their roles as fathers. They truly do become deadbeat dads.[4]

Can Drugs Be a Solution?

In inner-city neighborhoods and other economically deprived areas, teen fathers facing child support obligations they can't meet sometimes seek another sort of solution to their dilemma. Rather than walk away from the problem—and from their child—they turn to criminal activities as a way of getting money. Usually, this means the illegal drug trade.

Drugs are the horror of economically deprived areas. Sadly, they are often a major source of bringing money into these areas. There would seem to be endless opportunities for young men to deal drugs in poor neighborhoods. Some of these drugs are for use in the neighborhood, but a great deal are sold to better-off people who come there specifically to buy drugs. There is a constant need by higher-ups in the drug trade for faces new to the police to handle street sales. Race and color—still barriers in too many workplaces—are not discriminated against. The illegal drug kingpins are equal opportunity employers who don't care when that equal opportunity lands their young street hustlers in jail.

According to a 1996 study published in the *Families in Society* journal, there are two schools of thought about teen fathers who sell drugs. One "suggests that fathers who use or sell drugs are less likely to maintain contact with the mother and child because of the nature of their lifestyle. An alternative argument is that fathers who sell drugs may be more likely to maintain contact because they have an income that can be used to help support the family."[5]

The down side of that second possibility is that involvement in the drug trade invariably leads not only to jail, but to drug use as well. When teen fathers use drugs, the women they are involved with may join them. Too often, they are the teen mothers. The prospects for a child being well cared for in such a situation are not good. Using and dealing drugs are crimes, which lead to arrest, conviction, and imprisonment; given the harshness of the drug laws, prison sentences can keep a father from his child for long periods of time.

Families May Help

Not all teen fathers are faced with such difficult choices. Many have families, including low-income families, who will help out with the teen parents' finances. The teen dad's grand-parents, as well as his parents, may contribute. Even aunts and uncles may want to help out. In many cultures the family regards the birth of a child as a blessing, regardless of the age of the parents or the lack of marriage vows.

Financial aid may also come from the teen mother's family. They may agree to let her and the new baby live with them, and this will go a long way toward relieving the money problems. However, that's only a short-term solution. Whether or not the teen parents marry, or even agree to live together, sooner or later the mother and child will want to have their own place. Even if her family continues to help her, the teen father will still have an obligation to support his child.

The problems the teen father faces in accepting help from his own family, or the family of the teen mother, are the emotional conflicts, which inevitably arise from both the giving and the taking. The time may come when his gratitude will turn to guilt for taking money his family needs. They may resent him for accepting it. Her family may resent him even more bitterly as the cause of the additional expenses they are undergoing for their daughter and grandchild. There may be quarrels with families, and between teen father and teen mother as well. These will not create a healthy atmosphere for raising a child. However, being aware in advance of how these feelings of guilt,

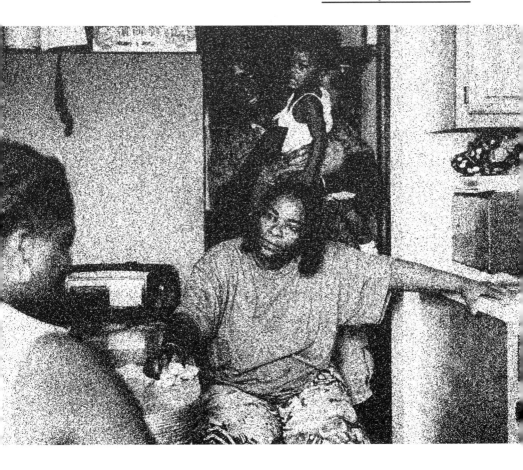

resentment, and bitterness arise may be useful in dealing with them in such a way as to defuse anger and keep family quarrels from growing into feuds. The quarrels may be about money, but they are also about more than money.

The Hidden Payback

This is most obvious in cases where the teen parents come from a middle-class or well-off background rather than from one that is economically deprived. The teen father who falls back on his family for financial aid may be protecting his future, but he is also shaping it in ways he may regret.

Fathering a child has pushed him—however unintentionally—into adulthood, but relying on his family to bail him out on an ongoing basis can push him right back into the dependency of an adolescent being supported by his parents.

That's the downside. The upside of such an arrangement for middle-class and upper-class teen dads is summed up by William Marsiglio in a study published in the 1995 issue of *Marriage & Family Review.* "The level and type of support young men receive from family members and friends may enable them to make certain choices about their education, work, and social life," writes Marsiglio. "These choices will have implications not only for the way they express themselves as fathers, but their partner's and children's life experiences as well. For instance, when grandparents of a young father's child provide financial and child care support, a young father (and his partner) may have the chance to further his education prior to seeking full-time employment without compromising his child's well-being. Consequently, his long-term potential to provide for his child may be enhanced."[6]

Of course, providing support for his child in the long term is most important for the teen dad. It sets up the conditions for an ongoing relationship with the child no matter how permanent or impermanent the relationship between the teen parents is. At the same time, it may be difficult to function as a father when one's lifestyle remains that of a child being cared for by his parents.

Arthur, now nineteen years old and the parent of a three-year-old son, has mixed feelings about the pros and cons of living with his family and being supported by them. He sees his son, David, often, but his relationship with the boy's mother, Marcy, has ended and she is involved with someone else. "The thing is that while she was with David all the time and being a mother to him, I was still living with my parents and in a lot of ways still being treated like a kid. It's not all their fault. I accepted it. But when Marcy said I was immature, I knew she was right. My son was an emotional kick, and I felt—still feel—responsible for him. But I wasn't being responsible. My parents were. The money wasn't important to them. I didn't think it was important to me, but it turns out it is. I'm glad I'm in college now so in the future I can support David. But I'm still being supported myself, and I just can't feel good about that."[7]

Obviously, Arthur's dilemma involves more than just money itself. It's the mixed feelings that the acceptance of money, or the lack of money, bring to the surface that so often positions the teen father between a rock and a hard place. A wise psychoanalyst once pointed out that in dealing with patients' problems sex was easy; it was money that was really hard. The truth of that, as we shall see in the next chapter, is too often demonstrated in the conflicts between teen fathers and the mothers of their children.

5.
FAMILY FRICTION

"All I heard from Lisa was, 'A man's supposed to do this. A man's supposed to do that.' I was living at home, working for my father. I was still in school."[1]
—Anthony, who became a father at age fifteen

People who don't have enough money argue about money more than people who do. Young men and young women may have very different priorities when it come to spending their limited finances.

"We don't agree on spending the money." It's a major problem for teen parents Janita, who is sixteen years old, and Elijah who is nineteen. "He goes to the supermarket and picks everything. He won't look at things and compare. He just spends money. I look for the cheap one that's just as good. We argue about that."[2]

The arguments inevitably carry over to how much should, and how much should not, be spent on their child. "The other day he bought the baby a bib that cost four dollars," sighs Janita. "I didn't get mad, but I told him, 'You're very dumb for doing that because we could have gotten two for that price.'"[3]

Elijah isn't dumb. Probably, he's just inexperienced. In many subcultures the mothers of the teen girls take them shopping for food and other items and teach them how to get value for their money. Teen males may not have had that experience. They simply aren't as knowledgeable or practical about household shopping as young women.

The Price of Being Broke

Of course it isn't always that cut and dried. When it comes to money there are as many issues having to do with the youth of teen parents as with their gender. They have spending patterns which predate their parenthood. They have expectations, which they can no longer afford to fulfill. This is as true of teen mothers as it is of teen fathers.

The teen mother may have been dating when she was younger. Perhaps she was used to boys paying for movies and pizza. Perhaps she was on an allowance, which allowed her to buy a sweater or a blouse when she felt like it. Perhaps she was brought up to believe that caring for the child and the home was the woman's job while supporting the mother and child was the man's job. Perhaps the father of her baby falls sadly short of these expectations.

He, of course, has his own experience and his own expectations. Once he was free to hang out with the guys, spend his money on impulse, not have to account to a girlfriend for where it went. Now his allowance and his part-time salary together barely cover his fatherhood expenses. There's no money to go bowling, to shoot a game of pool, or visit the video arcade.

A teen father and mother learn together that a baby is expensive and the knowledge too often brings resentment toward each other. The resentment leads to conflict, which leads to argument, which can lead to lasting bitterness. When the teen father is unable to supply enough money, the mother may feel he is pulling away, trying to extricate himself from the problems surrounding her and their baby. Sadly, that is sometimes the case. Even when it is not, the mother may feel neglected, even abandoned, while the teen father may feel cornered, trapped in a situation he is helpless to improve.

Concern or Domination?

Such money problems are often made worse by the involvement of the teen parents' families. One out of every ten teen fathers lives with his child's grandparents. In most cases, that means living with the mother's family.

His status in that household is often shaky. Even when his fatherhood role has been accepted, questions of how well or badly he is meeting his financial responsibilities are often at issue. If he and the baby's mother are quarreling about money, the argument inevitably spills over into a family discussion in which he finds himself in the minority.

He is still in his teens; his resources are limited; he has good reasons for not being able to meet his financial responsibilities. However, his wife and his child are at least partially dependent on her family for a roof over their heads, and sometimes for food and clothing as well. It's natural that the family feels that gives them the right to question how the teen parents spend their money. Once they have a say in the young people's finances, it follows that they will become involved in other aspects of their lives. This may not be done maliciously. Indeed, it may spring from love rather than resentment. However, for a teen father trying to establish his manhood by supporting his family, such interference often feels like domination.

The Pressure to Marry

Interference from the young mother's family often begins with the pressure to get married. The relatives of the pregnant teen will often push marriage as the way out of what they feel is a shameful situation. They lean on the girl and she leans on the teen father. Many young fathers are reluctant to be pushed into marriage, and statistically, their reluctance is justified. While *Family Planning Perspectives* has reported that "about one-third of unmarried young men who fathered children as teenagers married the mother within a year of the birth," more than six out of ten of these teen marriages last less than five years. The fact is that teen parents under the age of eighteen who marry are three times as likely to divorce as parents who marry when they are over the age of twenty-two.[4]

Families of teen parents who push marriage may offer persuasive counterarguments. According to the *American Sociological Review,* "married men live longer, drink less, take fewer risks, are more satisfied with life, and have higher incomes, educational attainments, and labor force attachments than unmarried men." Nevertheless, "unwed fathers are less likely to marry and more likely to cohabit [live with the mother of their child] than men without children before marriage."[5]

At age nineteen, Zachary is the father of a fourteen-month-old daughter. He expresses what many teen fathers feel about marriage. "Rachel wants to get married. I don't know if I'm ready. I'm playing it by ear. I'm more ready to be a father than a husband. . . . I know that I love her, and I'm sure I'll love her down the road. I also know that people change, and the divorce rate is really high."[6]

Who Does What, and When?

Whether the teen father marries the teen mother or lives with her and their child and her family, other conflicts besides those involving marriage and money will present themselves. The division of labor will probably lead the list. Who changes the baby? Gives it the two A.M. feeding? Takes it to the playground? Who does the cooking? The cleaning? The dishes? Who gets a night off, and when? What are the responsibilities of the teen mother in her parents' house? How many of those responsibilities should the teen father be expected to share?

Long-term planning might mean that he is completing his schooling as well as holding a part-time job. Can he study and work and share household duties and child care as well? If his wife is the one in school, or working, how much of the burden should shift onto his shoulders? And then there is the thorniest question of all: How much of a say should her family—the family he is living with—have in deciding such matters?

It is their home. Their daughter is an adolescent. She may be a mother herself now, but it's hard for them to stop treating her as one. She has lived by their rules and the rules are usually still there when the teen father moves into their home. The girl's parents may feel that those rules should apply to him as well. After all, they may feel, he too is not yet an adult.

The catch is that the demands of paternity are adult demands. He can't be expected to work, and perhaps go to school, and change the baby's diapers and then be told to be home at a certain hour or he's grounded. It may be too much to expect him to adapt to fatherhood and conform to rules laid down by his child's grandparents at the same time.

Responsibilities and Discipline

Another source of conflict is the different attitudes that the teen father and the teen mother and her family may have toward the child. Surveys of teen fathers repeatedly reveal that although "many fathers are willing to participate with the mother in the life of their child . . . their knowledge of child development is meager and their expectations of children are often unrealistic." As mentioned in Chapter Three, they view their parental responsibility as playing with the child, taking the child to the doctor, and disciplining the child, but most teen fathers do not believe that bathing the child and changing its diapers should be their responsibility.[7]

These attitudes do not usually agree with those of the mother who, as a rule, is the day-to-day caretaker of the child. Her daily experience has taught her the need to be patient and indulgent. Her more constant contact has put her in closer touch with the child's rhythms and rate of progress than the teen father. As the child grows older, she senses when the child is ready to handle simple orders, and knows that he or she may disobey because of lack of understanding, rather than due to willful defiance.

For many reasons the teen father may not connect with his child in this way—at least not at first. Nevertheless, a 1996 study published in the *Families in Society* journal found that teen fathers "saw themselves as becoming the primary disciplinarians of their children in the future." But how well prepared are they to take on that role? Too often strictness may be confused with discipline. Impatience and frustration can erupt into hitting or even worse, violence. Too often the teen father will believe that discipline means treating his child as he was treated and if that included mild or not so mild battering, then the pattern will continue. Training for teen fathers in relationship to discipline is available from a variety of organizations and will be discussed in a later chapter.[8]

Fathers Are Important

Discipline may involve pitfalls, but at the same time it testifies to the strong desire of teen fathers to be involved with their child. The study published in *Family in Society* found two possible reasons why this is expressed as an emphasis on discipline. One was a determination by teen fathers to counteract what they saw as overindulgence of their child by the child's mother and/or family. Another had to do with the fact that many teen fathers had themselves "grown up in single-female headed households." They had mixed feelings about this, which led to them believing that "it was particularly important for male children to have their fathers involved with them throughout their lives." They believed that their child needed a strong father figure, and "strong" often translated as discipline.[9]

One of the teen fathers in the study, GK, put the view widely held by the other teen fathers into words. "I think fathers are important, especially for boys," he affirmed. "Every child needs a role model; boys need fathers as models."[10]

Another young father, MM, explained his feelings of fatherlessness and how they made him feel toward his own child:

"My mom and my grandmother raised me. My dad? All I know is his name . . . and when I was about [his own child's] age he left my mom. So, my mind-set is that I want to be everything that he wasn't to me. Meanin' I want to be something to my son. I want to be a [cherished] memory, I don't want to be like just a name. My mom was talkin' about finding my dad, and I was like, 'Well, go ahead . . . I don't care.' I don't want to be like that with [his own child]. I want to be

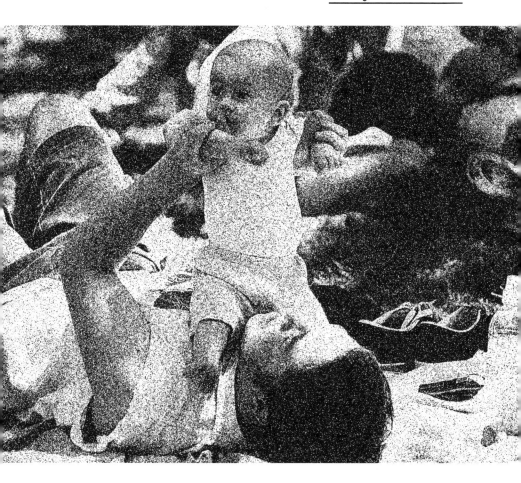

part of his life. I want him to say, 'My dad is right there.' I want to take him to ball games, I want to keep him strong, I want to be his life."[11]

Leaving, Not Deserting

That's not always easy. As the baby becomes a toddler and the toddler a child, the pressures increase on the teen father. The conflicts heat up. There are fights and arguments with his child's mother about money, discipline, and the division of labor. Free time is an issue. There is never enough time left over after doing everything that has to be done. Living in close proximity under these conditions can breed dissatisfaction with one another. The young woman's family sides with her. Other relatives and family friends line up against him—or so it seems. He is a stranger in the house, and perhaps an unwelcome one at that. He decides he must leave.

This doesn't end his involvement with his child. A survey of teen dads covering eight locations was conducted by the Young Unwed Fathers Program (YUPF) and reported by *Welfare Information Network.* It indicated that "39 percent of fathers not living with their children saw them almost every day and 70 percent saw their children at least once a week. Over half of the fathers surveyed reported taking their children to the doctor, or dressing, feeding, and playing with their children."[12]

Unfortunately, leaving doesn't always ease the conflicts with the child's mother and her family, either. Simply trying to arrange visits with his child may run into resistance. Friction between the teen father and mother may even grow worse after he leaves. Again, there is the feeling of desertion on one side and the feeling of being ostracized and excluded on the other.

Teen father DC describes a typical result: "Well, like when me and [partner] weren't fond of each other, it kept me and my son apart. She would always [say], 'I don't want to see you today,' or I would want to see my son, and me and her were fightin', I would say, 'Well, I'm comin' over' . . . and she'd say, 'No, you don't,' and leave. And I would come over there and she'd be gone."

Another young father described how after trying and trying to see his child and his child's mother, he was chased at gunpoint from her family's house by her relatives.[13]

Obstacles and Feelings

Things may not play out so dramatically, but living apart from the child and mother along with the simple day-to-day effort of keeping up contact in what can be a hostile atmosphere can wear the teen father down. And then, of course, there are the holidays. He wants to share them with his child, but too often he feels like an intruder.

On Thanksgiving he finds himself eating turkey with people who may not want him to be there. On Christmas, or Hanukkah, or the holidays of other religions, his gifts to his child may be judged by their cost rather than by the value of the love which accompanies them. The seven days of Kwanzaa, a holiday celebrated by some African Americans to celebrate the blessings of the past season (and isn't his child one of those blessings?) may be a period of strain if joy in the child is mixed with resentment at the father's presence.

Timing is always a problem. The father must time his visits to the schedule of the child's mother and her family. If they have weekend plans, he may not get to see his child. If they go away on vacation, it may be weeks, even a month, and children grow so fast. He feels like his child is slipping away from him and he doesn't know what to do about it. Over time, such obstacles may wear him down. The young dad may put fatherhood on the back burner. He pays a psychological price for this—repressed anger, frustration, a sense of loss, defeat, guilt. Studies of absent fathers indicate that it is the obstacles to paternity that so often drive them away, not the lack of a sense of responsibility.

Institutional Roadblocks

Chief among these obstacles, many teen fathers say, is the attitude of the very social institutions that are set up to facilitate child care by young parents. They viewed the staffs of service agencies, hospitals, and schools as hostile to them—assigning blame—and biased in favor of their child's mother. They felt that rather than helping them, they too often hindered their child care efforts. Teen father GK relates an example of how teen fathers may be treated that is all too common:

> *"My son was seven months old, and he had a bite mark on his face. I asked [the baby's mother] who did it, and she said she didn't know. I asked her, did she take him [to the emergency room], 'cause at the time she was staying at a place where cats and dogs was, and I figured, well, if a dog or somethin' bit him, he should go in for shots. So I take him to the hospital. They look at*

*him and they document it and they tell me, 'Well,
maybe you oughta take him to St. Joe's [foster home
agency] and let them do some documents.' Well, I
made it to St. Joe's, they told me give 'em [child] and
I can go. And I'm thinkin', I'm bringin' my son here,
I want to know what's goin' on. They tell me, 'We
can't.'*

"*When I call up there or when I went back there,
they tell me I can't even see my son. They took him
and told me, 'Even though you're the father we can't
tell you nothing. We have to notify the mother, let her
know her son is here, let her know who brought him.'
Even though I'm the one who brought him. Later,
when I asked the county about the report concerning
the bite marks, they told me, 'We can't tell you anything; that information is confidential.' GK paused,
looking puzzled. "I'm the one who made the report.*"[14]

Adoption and Options

The pressures of teen parents living separately aren't one-
sided. The teen mother may find that while the leaving of the
teen father has relieved the tension around the house, it has also
deprived her of support in navigating her dual role as both
mother and child. Sometimes the pressures overwhelm her. She
and the teen father had agreed to have the baby and bring it up,
but now he is not a constant presence and the burden is on her.
It is too much. She wants to have her own life. She talks it over
with her parents and the decision is made. The child will be
given up for adoption.

The young father is outraged. It's hard enough now maintaining regular contact with his child. If it is adopted who knows
if he will ever see it again? He fears losing all contact. The alternative is for him to take the child and rear it himself. Can he do
that? What are his rights? Does he have any?

If he is able to care for the child himself as an alternative to
adoption, it comes down to whether he can establish his legal
custody over the child, and to whether the child's mother will

agree to his having such custody or, perhaps, to sharing custody with him. Unfortunately, there is no clear-cut pattern when it comes to young fathers getting custody. One study found that they were successful in 63 percent of cases where they pursued custody, while another concluded that mothers were granted custody twice as often as fathers.

The Changing Custody Laws

Custody laws have been constantly changing over the years. It was not so long ago that they favored fathers—even young fathers—on the grounds that they would be better able to provide financial support than mothers, particularly young unwed mothers. However, as women claimed their rights in other areas of life, a recognition of their value as caretakers who mold children became recognized. The pendulum swung and the law began to view motherhood rather than fatherhood as in the best interest of the child when choices had to be made.

During the 1970s, fathers' rights groups sprang up to protest discrimination against fathers in custody disputes. This led to reform. Today most state custody laws forbid taking the sex of either parent into consideration in custody cases. However, the argument continues. Some advocates for young mothers argue that since young men really are in a position to earn more child support money than young women, not taking the sex of the parent into account means minimizing the value of the mother's role and favoring the father for economic reasons.

They would seem to be winning their case. Custody is still mostly awarded to mothers. However, there is an increasing trend toward awarding joint custody to young parents. This means that while the child goes on living with the mother, the teen father has equal decision-making powers where his offspring is concerned. One thought behind this is that he will be more likely to make support payments if he has a say in his child's upbringing.

In California, 79 percent of the cases where custody is at issue are resolved by joint legal custody. Indeed, joint custody was granted in 32 percent of the cases where the mother's request for custody was not contested by the father. For the teen father involved in seeking custody a joint legal custody outcome is more likely when he works with an attorney. Free legal aid may be available to him through one of the support services covered in Chapter Nine. If he is trying to prevent his child being put up for adoption, such professional help will be necessary.

Mediation: Pro and Con

Many experts believe that joint custody falls far short of an ideal solution, particularly when there is hostility between young parents. They view it as a compromise between parents who can't get along and believe that over time it may only give rise to greater hostility. Sometimes they see it as exposing the child to continuing parental conflict. The evidence is that such children may suffer from depression, express deviant behavior, and exhibit other symptoms of maladjustment.

Trying to prevent matters from reaching this point, some states have passed mandatory mediation laws for parents who have separated. Such laws apply to never-married fathers, including teen fathers. One of their goals is to ensure fathers' visitation rights. However, mediation has its downside. Where child abuse or wife abuse is involved, the abuser may dominate the process and come out on top. For this reason, some states have excluded abusers and abused spouses from the mediation process. Indeed, many moderators have come to believe that mediation always produces a result in favor of the more dominant partner. Their experience has been that the result is inevitable because the commitment is to resolving the dispute, and not necessarily to arriving at a fair result.

These are heavy considerations for a father still himself in his teens. There are questions he must ask himself. Will raising the child himself be in the child's best interest? What will it mean to the child to be raised by an unwed father? Is it possible to share custody with his child's mother without ongoing conflict that will harm the child?

Not so long ago unwed fathers had few if any rights concerning their offspring. They had no standing to prevent an adoption. Today, however, several Supreme Court decisions have changed that. Unmarried fathers today do have legal rights. The question is how well they will—or will not—use them.

6.
BACKGROUND TO PATERNITY

". . . I don't think of them as my kids. . . . If the girl gets pregnant, then they are hers. That's the way my people are."[1]

—Carlos, now nineteen years old.
The first of Carlos's nine out-of-wedlock
children was born when he was twelve.

The conflicts between teen fathers and teen mothers and their families often have their origins in their ethnic, religious, and racial backgrounds. This is true even when both of them come from the same background. Their backgrounds may be sources of pride for them, and for their families, but they also may include attitudes which cause disputes when it comes to money, sex, marriage, and the raising of children.

According to the National Center for Health Statistics (NCHS) of the U.S. Department of Health and Human Services, "the majority of teen mothers are white." They and the fathers of their children—mostly teen fathers—come from a variety of ethnic backgrounds within that racial category. "In 1995 (the latest year for which statistics are available), 355,489 babies were born to white teens." By contrast, "139,621 babies were born to blacks (teens); 9,038 to teens of Asian or Pacific Island descent; and 7,967 to Native Americans. Included in these figures are 121,636 babies born to Hispanic teens, who are not classified as a separate racial group in NCHS data." As with whites, there are many subgroups within these categories.[2]

The attitudes of these subgroups may be reflected by the rates of births to teens in some of the countries represented in their backgrounds. A 1997 study shows that while there are only four births per thousand for females between the ages of fifteen and nineteen in Japan, nine per thousand in France, and twenty-three per thousand in Austria, in the United States there are fifty-seven such births per thousand. The United States teen birthrate is the highest in the industrialized world. The United Kingdom, which comes second, is not even close with thirty-two births per thousand to teens in that age group.

Different Cultures, Similar Attitudes

Immigrants' attitudes toward teen parenthood and the issues surrounding it generally carry over from their country of origin to the United States. However, these attitudes soften as families assimilate into the mainstream. Families may also be less judgmental and more accepting as they move up the economic ladder. Even when such attitudes remain unchanged, for second- and third-generation Americans the degree to which they are enforced is usually not as harsh as it was by those who came before them.

What is striking is the similarities in the way teen parenthood is regarded by cultures that may seem very different from one another in other ways. "For an Italian father," says Alberto, who emigrated to the United States from Sicily, "for a teen daughter to get pregnant is a stain upon his honor, which can only be erased by the boy marrying her no matter how young they are. If there is no marriage there will be bad blood between the families. For Italians in the United States it is maybe not so cut and dried. Maybe they don't marry, but there is a responsibility and the boy must accept it. One way or another, he must pay. There must be an arrangement of satisfaction to both families."[3]

This is not very different from the attitudes Emilio, a recent immigrant from the Philippines, reports as common in the Philippine-American community, which has established itself on New York City's East Side. "Very bad," he says. "A young boy who gets a young girl with child disgraces his people—his parents, his family, his village, or in the United States it is perhaps just the neighborhood. They have to marry right away and either families set them up with a home, or they live with relatives. But when they do that, they never hear the end of it."[4]

How is it that Filipino attitudes and Italian attitudes are so similar? "Both nationalities are Catholic," is the reason in Giorgio's opinion. "The Church is very strict about kids not having sex until they get married." However, many other religions take an equally dim view of teen sex. Fundamentalist Protestants, Orthodox Jews, and Muslims all regard adolescents who have sex as sinful and—at the very least—believe that pregnancy which precedes marriage should be followed by it.[5]

Macho Teen Fatherhood

In Latino families, which are also largely Roman Catholic, the morality involves a more macho reaction to teen parenthood. Traditionally, the more children a Latino male has, the more of a man he is thought to be. However, the Hispanic teen girl who becomes pregnant, like the Italian girl and the Filipino girl in similar circumstances, has disgraced her family and may be thrown out of her home. The teen father's family is not regarded as dishonored. On the contrary, his paternity is regarded as "confirmation of his virility (masculinity)."[6]

It's not surprising then that "Hispanic boys begin having intercourse at earlier ages than their white counterparts. In a study of fifty-six adolescent fathers in Albuquerque [New Mexico], Hispanic men were more likely to become fathers before age eighteen and reported a larger range of problems relating to parenthood than either Anglo or black men."[7]

According to studies by the Alan Guttmacher Institute, "Hispanic-American youth who are sexually active are infrequent and unskilled users of contraceptives. Among teenagers engaging in sexual intercourse, Hispanic-American young women are less likely to use contraception than their Anglo-American counterparts. The relatively high rate of sexual involvement in Hispanic males and the relatively low rate of effective contraceptive use by sexually active Hispanic teenagers help to explain the relatively high teenage pregnancy rates among Hispanics."[8]

Traditionally, if not too consistently, the Hispanic teen father comes "under strong pressure to marry the mother and set up another household with her and the baby." However, for many Hispanics, the money isn't there for a second household. Marriage often means the teen father must move in with his wife's family. More and more, as Hispanics are assimilated into the American culture, he may live with them without marrying the mother of his child.[9]

It should be noted that the problem with such studies as those cited above is that they tend to lump all Hispanics together. In reality, there are many different Hispanic cultures in the United States—Mexican-American, Puerto Rican-American, Dominican-American, Cuban-American, and so forth. There may be differences among them in attitudes toward teen parenthood, as in other areas. Until there are studies of each group, conclusions about Hispanics generally should be regarded with caution. The high birthrate among Hispanic teens is more related to their lower than average economic status than it is to their ethnic background.

The heritage of most white and black teen parents is northern European or African, not Latino. Their religion is for the most part Protestant or Muslim, not Roman Catholic. However, they too are more likely to be from the poorest segment of their respective races. Likewise, it is only the most economically deprived Asian-American adolescents and teenage Americans from the Pacific Islands, with a teen birthrate less than half that of the national average, who become teen parents. It's lack of money that fuels the teen parent problem, and in the inner cities of the United States, that mostly means Hispanics and African Americans.

African-American Responsibility

As we have seen, there are many more white teen parents than black teen parents. Nevertheless, the percentage rate of teen births for blacks, while decreasing, is still double that for whites. Surveys of inner cities where poor blacks are in the majority show that African-American and Caribbean-American male teens usually acknowledge their paternity. In the journal of *Marriage & Family Review,* sociologist-author William Marsiglio notes that "the black community frequently supports young fathers' participation in informal child support/care arrangements." Referring to a National Urban League study, he also reports that "in recent years, the black middle class has supplemented these informal efforts by attempting to marshal community support for its campaign to encourage young black men, especially those living in central city areas, to interact with their partners and children in a more responsible manner."[10]

Family Planning Perspectives has reported that only 15 percent of black teen fathers live with their child as opposed to 60 percent of economically disadvantaged whites and 80 percent of higher income whites. However, compiling evidence from many studies, Paul and Susan S. Lang concluded in their book *Teen Fathers* that "two-thirds of the black teenage fathers studied saw their child at least every other day." Some sociologists have concluded that both the greater acceptance of out-of-wedlock teen births and the frequency of teen fathers living apart from their children are a legacy from slavery times. Whether this is so or not, teen births may well be handled with less stress by black families than others.[11]

On the other hand, African-American and Caribbean-American families may tend to be more involved with their teenagers' offspring than other ethnic groups. This can be a two-edged sword. As desirable as acceptance and love may be, interference with child rearing can lead to friction. Indeed, even noninterference, interpreted as over-permissiveness, can cause resentment.

"My father, my mother, my sisters, and my girlfriend's mother, sisters, and aunts treat Andre like he was their child," reports Andre's father, sixteen-year-old Kenyatta. "Sometimes we have to let them know that we're the parents. He's so young, sometimes he starts to run and bang things up and the relatives just laugh. They think it's funny. I know he's a baby, but he has to know what he can't do, or else when he's older, he'll terrorize people. Now he thinks, 'Auntie or Grandma won't stop me.' So I have to stop him."[12]

In Search of Closeness

Kenyatta's desire to be involved with his child is typical of teen fathers who did not have relationships with their own fathers. In one recent study, 50 percent of the teen fathers interviewed complained of not having an adequate father figure to whom they could relate while they were growing up. Researchers at the Alan Guttmacher Institute believe that "emotional deprivation at an early age, leading teens to seek closeness through sexual relations or parenting, has been implicated in premature pregnancy."[13] Others in the field speculate that the young father's lack of a relationship with his own father may sometimes prompt him to deliberately father a child in order to offer it the kind of parenting, from a male, which he never had.

At the same time, African-American teen fathers are more likely than other teen males to be children of teenage parents themselves, to have a sibling born out of wedlock, or to have a sibling who was an unwed parent. They are more likely to have peers and family members who consider adolescent parenthood nonjudgmentally—even with approval. Teen parenting is a way of life they know even when their fathers are absent, and they are often eager to become fathers themselves.

When they do, however, they risk repeating the pattern set up by their own absent fathers. The evidence is that "parent-child relationships are formed early in children's lives and are important to their social, psychological, emotional and

behavioral development and well-being. When one parent is not involved, which in most cases is the father . . . there are noticeable negative effects. . . . Children without fathers are three times more likely to fail at school, to experience emotional or behavioral problems requiring psychiatric treatment, and to commit suicide as adolescents." Even when that is not the case, "a father's involvement is important for other reasons, including nurturance, lifting children out of poverty, and enhancing children's mental and physical well being."[14]

Dads in Jail

That involvement is too often lacking. Four out of every ten children in the United States are not living in the same home as their biological father. In a large number of these cases the missing father is African American or Hispanic American. Where are these much needed missing fathers whose teen sons are becoming fathers themselves? A great many of them are in the hands of the criminal justice system—either in jail or awaiting sentencing or out on parole.

According to Amnesty International, of the more than 1.7 million people in prisons or jails in the United States, more than 60 percent are from racial or ethnic minorities, and over half are African American. The Sentencing Project, a Washington D.C.-based public advocacy group "warns that more African-Americans than ever are being locked up in America's prisons." It projects that "if present trends continue one million African-American adults, mostly young black males, will wind up behind bars by the end of the year 2000."[15]

Director of the National Center on Institutions and Alternatives, Jerome G. Miller, points out that almost three quarters of new admissions to prisons are African American or Hispanic. He predicts that by 2010, "we will have the absolute majority of all African-American males between age eighteen and forty in prisons and camps."[16] It has been estimated elsewhere that 64 percent of these minority male prisoners are fathers!

High rates of imprisonment for minority males, particularly African-American and Hispanic teens, are blamed on a variety of factors by those who have studied the problem. Poverty and lack of employment opportunities head a list, which also accuses police of racial profiling and targeting minority youth. The charge is made that both police and the courts enforce drug laws strictly in black and Hispanic neighborhoods where crack cocaine is the drug of choice, while ignoring white suburban use of substances like powder cocaine and marijuana. It is also charged that minorities routinely receive harsher sentences than white middle-class males. The fact is that the vast majority of minority men in prison are there for nonviolent, and usually drug-related, crimes.

Battered by Poverty

These black and Hispanic prisoners are both the fathers of teen fathers and, sometimes, teen fathers themselves. The need to rehabilitate them and restore their relationships to their children is key to dealing with the problems of teen fatherhood. According to studies by the Welfare Information Network, "the two best predictors of whether incarcerated males will continue to commit more crimes after they are released are religion and family." These studies indicate that like the majority of teen fathers who are not in jail, "criminals are overwhelmingly males who grew up without fathers." They need to be taught parenting skills.[17]

The teaching of such skills may have to begin with changing the attitudes of teen fathers from economically deprived households. Poverty is frustrating. It raises tempers. The outlet for suppressed rage is too often the family. Adolescent fathers generally have been found to be more physically abusive toward their children than older fathers. The frustration of not having enough money makes child battering an even more likely possibility for fathers in their teens.

A side effect of this is that teen fathers are also more likely than older fathers to end up as defendants in family court. This too is part of the cycle of poverty surrounding teen fatherhood, and it is as true for whites as it is for blacks. Ethnic, racial, and cultural influences may play a part, but the bottom line is that the problems of teen fatherhood among minorities are most deeply rooted in poverty. It follows that alleviating poverty may be the best way to discourage teen fatherhood.

7.
DIFFERENT HERITAGES

"I'm Native American and Jessica's white. Jessica's mom says I'm going to be a fat, lazy drunk, and I'm going to beat her and beat my son. That's not the case at all."[1]
—Teen father Michael, nineteen years old, has a one-year-old son, and his girlfriend, Jessica, is pregnant with their second child.

Marriage across racial, ethnic, and religious lines has been occurring more and more often in the United States over the past ten years. This is also true of marital and nonmarital relationships involving teens. For teen fathers like Michael it is one more pressure to be dealt with in addition to all the others. Despite the increase in cross-cultural relationships, including those resulting in paternity, negative attitudes toward them are not changing at the same pace.

While recent surveys of teen males indicate that close to 50 percent don't think it matters if the person they are involved with has a different group background from their own, their attitude changes when the question is asked as to whether this might cause a problem in a co-parenting or a marriage situation. Over 30 percent of those who felt a different background would make no difference to them felt that it would cause problems if there was a child. They felt that these problems would not necessarily originate with the teen father or mother, but rather with their families. The teen fathers expressed concern that as their children grew up, they might be discriminated against by peers and by society in general if they came from two different backgrounds.

Ethnic Pride: A Victim

At the root of such discrimination are family attitudes. In many households, ethnic pride is expressed in terms of being "better" than other cultures, or set apart from them. An unintended pregnancy involving an outsider may be viewed as an assault on the basic identity of the family.

"La familia!" Andy is the eighteen-year-old son of divorced working parents in Tucson, Arizona. He is also the unmarried father of one-year-old Miguel. Andy is from a mixed European-American background. Miguel's mother, Inez, is Mexican American. "The family." Andy is bitter. "Because they have property and money and were here before the Anglos, they believe they are so superior. For them it's like I have nothing to do with Miguel being here. They don't bend. They don't give an inch."[2]

Yet on the face of it, that isn't really true. Inez's family seems to fully accept Miguel. Indeed, Inez's mother and her aunts dote on the child. The men of her family provide for Inez and Miguel. They are polite but cold with Andy. He is the father of Inez's child. They have accepted that. But he is not one of them. They allow him certain privileges, but they restrict him as well. Once Andy overheard a brother refer to him contemptuously as "that Anglo."

"I can see Inez and Miguel. I can even sleep over. But somehow they arrange it so that I can never be alone with the mother of my child. I think they're afraid we'll have sex and make another baby. Sometimes I think, maybe we should, just to let them know I'm here. Still here. Not going anywhere."[3]

Andy would like to marry Inez, to take her and Miguel off to a home of their own. He is receiving training as an automobile mechanic and working in an auto shop. "We couldn't live the way she lives now," he concedes. "But at least we'd be out from under them."[4]

An Unresolved Issue

Religion is an issue, perhaps a weapon. When Inez first became pregnant her family, which is instrumental in maintaining the local Catholic mission church, sought counseling from the priest in charge, who was also a family friend. Subsequently, at their request, the priest met with Andy. "We talked about me converting to Catholic," Andy recalls. "I wasn't brought up religiously and I had no particular objection if it was going to make things easier. See, back then I thought we'd get married, me and Inez."[5]

Her family prevented the marriage. The priest didn't think that Andy was ready to convert, or had any genuine commitment to becoming a Catholic. The family could not accept a marriage outside the Church for their daughter. Miguel was born and the situation remains unresolved.

Andy fears that they are seeking a way to resolve it that will exclude him. He sees Miguel fairly regularly now, and has been bonding with him. To Andy, however, the closeness with Inez seems to be fading. He can't put his finger on it, fears he may be getting paranoid. His nightmare is that they'll find some *hidalgo*—upper-class Mexican American—to marry Inez and take over fatherhood of Miguel. He doesn't want to lose his son, but the weight of culture and tradition posed against him seems to Andy to be insurmountable.

The Compromised Heritage

Twenty-five percent of teen couples who live together live with a partner "from a different ethnic group or race" according to "Teen Expectations of and Realities in Marriage and Living Together," a survey of 3,728 teens conducted by 95 teachers and other professionals under the leadership of Teen Parent Program developer Jeanne Warren Lindsay. One in five of the males in such living arrangements said this "caused problems for themselves, and one in five said it was a problem for their parents." Teen parenthood makes the problems worse.[6]

The teen father brings his own ethnic, racial, religious, and class background to the situation. He is not free of his own pride, nor of his own sensitivities. Nor is he free of his own prejudices, even when they may be well below the surface of his awareness. When he accepts the role of teen father, whether it involves marriage or not, he will first be dealing with these feelings—these issues—in terms of the mother of his child, and probably her family. However, there will come a time when he must also confront them with his child.

He is a white man and his child is black. He is a Jew and his child is being raised as a Christian. He is Muslim and his child is not receiving instruction at the mosque. His child is being raised in a family that does not honor the pope, does not observe Ramadan, teaches machismo over serenity, or passivity over manliness. There arise issues of behavior, which stem from a heritage different from that of the teen father. And since the teen father is rarely in control, it too often seems that it is his values that are being sacrificed, and that alternate values of which he may not approve are being foisted on his child.

How shall he deal with this? How shall his child learn to love opera in a house where jazz is king? How will he learn to bow with dignity in a house where no one bends a knee? How will he learn to honor his father when all that is his father is put on the back burner? Shall the teen father fight to bring these values to his child? Will that only cause dissension? Will it confuse his child? Will trying to instill pride in his child's paternal background backfire and only push him deeper into the alternate culture in which he is being raised?

Painful Communication

The most difficult thing is bringing these issues out into the open where they can be discussed. There is touchiness on all ethnic, racial, and religious sides. To insist on one's own values too often comes across as an attack on the values of others. Still, communication must begin while the child is still young enough to be influenced, and usually that means communication with the child's mother.

Such communication can be painful. Nor does it always resolve anything, as Meghan and Justin, who became parents of two-and-a-half-year-old Jameka while still in their teens, have been finding out. For most of their daughter's life they have been trying to come to terms with their religious differences. Meghan, now eighteen years old, despairs that they ever will: "He's Catholic and I'm not," Meghan says. "It hasn't been a problem because he didn't go to church hardly ever. The only thing that bothered us was we would talk about getting married and he would want to do it in a Catholic church and I don't want to do that. You have to go through classes, and I didn't believe in that. That bothered me."[7]

Another couple, Jessica and Brad, fifteen-year-old parents of four-month-old Rodney, are similarly unable to resolve their religious differences. "We had a big argument about getting Rodney baptized," Jessica reports. "Brad wanted it done in his mom's church, and I said she doesn't even go. I wouldn't budge on that one." However, the problem went deeper than that. "He only went to church once with me. I wouldn't want to be with someone who could not respect my religion. I want my son to be brought up in a Christian life-style."[8]

Rodney is still an infant. What will happen if Jessica and Brad can't resolve their different attitudes toward religion? They are still very young, and what will happen with Rodney in terms of the heritage his father wishes him to have if they split up? Even assuming that Brad continues to see Rodney, how much of his own tradition will he be able to pass along to him? How much of it will be swamped by Rodney's everyday experiences with his mother and her family and their friends?

Outside Pressure

The issues extend beyond the family to the group. Movements to reaffirm racial, religious, and ethnic values are constantly proclaiming the obligation to embrace ones' roots and to insist on their validity in a world where everybody is, in some ways, a member of a minority. It's basic to such movements that their group values be instilled in the children born into the group. The problem for the teen dad, however, is that his child may be born into more than one group and that the struggle over which set of values he or she is to receive may pull the child in different directions.

Asa is a black Muslim who went on the Million Man March to Washington, D.C., when he was sixteen years old. He formed there a fierce pride in his African-American heritage. He wants his son Jabal to grow up knowing who he is, a black man with a noble history. He wants Jabal to be proud of being black. But Jabal's teen mother, who is raising him with the help of her family, is white, and the boy himself is not at first glance dark-skinned enough to be regarded as African American. There is Jabal's German-Irish heritage to consider as well—the songs his mother sings, the dishes she cooks, the stories his white relatives tell. Can Jabal take in both heritages and fuse them? Asa does not believe that's possible. He points out that for many black people having white blood is only proof of their forebears' victimization as slaves. Asa insists that Jabal must embrace being black, and the Nation of Islam stands firmly behind him.

It is not the only group standing guard over its flock. Others, concerned that intergroup relationships are eating away at the bedrock of their beliefs and that group members are drifting away, also implement programs of damage control. Fundamentalist Christians, Conservative Jewish organizations, and other religious groups have all mounted campaigns against intermarriage. These take an equally dim view of romances with people outside the faith, and of teenagers who parent children with someone not of their faith. At the same time, in the case of religious groups, just about all of them will accept the child into the fold if the parents will make a decision for the child to embrace the religion. Many will go beyond that and offer help and counseling for both teen parents and child. All that is asked is that the child be brought up in the particular religion of one of the teen parents. All that is asked of the other—usually the teen father—is that he agree to this and forego his own preference for his child.

Such demands are not limited to religious and racial groups. There are many nationally based ethnic groups which make similar claims to the allegiance of the children of teen parents. These run the gamut from Chinese American, Japanese American, and Korean American to Lakota and Sioux Americans, Armenian Americans and Polish Americans. Each ethnic group wants their culture to predominate with the children of teen parents. Each offers many benefits if that is allowed to happen. But each is asking a sacrifice. The price can be the teen father's right to have his son grow up identifying with his own racial, religious, or ethnic group. He has to ask himself if that is a price he is willing to pay.

A Different Outlook

The issues appear to be different for white middle-class teen fathers. There have not been many studies done on them, and most of the evidence regarding the problems and pressures they face is anecdotal, but family and status and image would seem to play more of a role than race, religion, or ethnicity. Absent the financial pressures on poor and minority teen fathers, they have more options, more ability to pursue long-term goals, but also more negative family attitudes toward teen fatherhood with which to contend. There is rarely the acceptance of the teen father role that is found, say, in the African-American community.

"Abortion." Remembering back to when he told his white, middle-class parents that Marcy was pregnant and he was responsible, Arthur remembers their immediate reaction. "To them it was the obvious solution to keep their teenage son on track. Their agenda for me was college, grad school, a career, and definitely no detours to play daddy. But oh, yeah, first a DNA test because maybe, just maybe, the baby wasn't really mine. Like I was the village idiot and Marcy had been sleeping around and was trying to pull a fast one and blame it on me. Only the truth is that Marcy comes from a suburban family pretty much like mine. They were outraged when DNA got mentioned."[9]

DNA is the unique genetic substance in body cells that is passed on from parent to child at conception. It makes it possible to establish the father of a child with close to absolute accuracy. Cornell University senior science writer Susan Lang and her associate Paul Lang report that "courts now routinely use this method to establish paternity, that is, legally identify the father." However, this option is rarely used in cases of teen parenthood. It may be that there is more trust on the part of the teens involved—particularly middle-class teens like Arthur and Marcy—than on the part of some of the middle-class parents.[10]

Staying the Course

The thrust of Arthur's parents' thinking was to find a way for him to avoid the burdens of fatherhood. When abortion was ruled out, they pushed to have the baby adopted immediately after birth. While there was conflict between them and Marcy's family, her parents also tended to view adoption as a solution. They wanted Marcy to continue her education without taking on the burden of teen motherhood. At this point neither set of parents was hearing what Arthur and Marcy were saying.

Arthur feels that the attitudes of both sets of parents was typical of their life situation and middle-class values. He also feels that they shut off emotionally in ways that Marcy and he did not. "It's like the baby had no reality for them," he remembers. "There was just this problem to be solved."[11]

Despite their parents' attitudes, Arthur and Marcy prevailed and David was born. He was not put up for adoption. Now three years old, he is being brought up by Marcy as a single mother living in her parents' house. Arthur sees him regularly and remains a devoted father.

At the same time, Arthur feels that he remains a prisoner of the middle-class attitudes of his parents. They contribute generously to David's support, but otherwise they barely acknowledge their grandson's existence. They treat Arthur as the nineteen-year-old college freshman he has become. Arthur feels that slowly but surely he is being eased into the role they have always had mapped out for him. He worries about what that's going to do to his relationship to David over the long haul.

Is the reaction of Arthur's parents typical of other white middle-class parents confronted with a teenage son's paternity? Are abortion and adoption the solutions for this group most of the time? Is there more of a need for the white middle class to sweep problems of teen paternity under the carpet? Are those in this group more reluctant to make emotional connections, no matter how embarrassing, than those in the other groups we have looked at?

The answer is that much more will have to be known before these questions can be answered. Beyond poverty, it has been said, the misfortune of the poor is to be surveyed, and surveyed again. We know a lot about how the less well-off ethnic groups handle teen fatherhood, but we don't really know much at all about how middle-class white families deal with it. Nobody is focusing studies of teen fatherhood on them. Perhaps it's time someone did.

8.
THIRD-PARTY RELATIONSHIPS

"Me and Angela are together, but I still find my eyes wandering. Sometimes I think, 'I'm just 18, why ain't I out there?' One of the big problems about having a relationship so young is you tend to regret it. You know you have to mature so quick."[1]

—Juan, eighteen, co-parent with Angela,
sixteen, of Vaneza, seven months.

No matter the commitment the teen father and mother start out with to each other, there may come a day when one, or both of them, feels differently. Their devotion to their child may stay strong, but their feelings toward each other may crumble under the pressures of their situation as teen parents. They may simply drift apart, or their separating may be more volatile than that. Difficult times follow and it isn't always easy for the teen father to balance them out against the welfare of his child.

It may begin with his having been pushed away by the teen mother's family, or by the mother herself. Perhaps an unwillingness to marry—his unwillingness, or hers—is at the root of their growing alienation from each other. Perhaps it is the teen father's own feeling of being trapped, hemmed in, forbidden to experience sex with other women as he would like to do before tying himself down to one woman and a family. This may not seem very mature, but then why should it be? Father or not, he really isn't quite grown up yet.

Making It Work: Tino and Donna

Most young fathers may experience feelings that they are missing something by tying themselves down to one relationship, but not all of them give in to those feelings. Some make a conscious and ongoing effort to work things out with the mother of their child. Teen Parent Program developer Jeanne Warren Lindsay presents one such case as an example of how a young father and young mother faced the problem and dealt with it.

Ms. Lindsay writes of Tino and Donna, who had their first child when they were both sixteen years old. By the time that child was nine years old, they had two other children together as well. Although not married, they have worked at maintaining their relationship over the years, and that has meant facing up to the possibility of other involvements. They recall that there came a point where Donna's sex drive had gone down while Tino's hadn't, and they made a conscious effort to go dancing and out to dinner to "keep the sex alive."

"Just doing something by yourselves helps keep the romance alive," Tino advises. "A lot of young people have to realize the grass is not greener on the other side. As long as you keep your own relationship watered and nurtured, it will be just as green—or even greener."

Donna agrees. "Maybe they see somebody they think is better, then they get a divorce, then they realize the next one is not better. It's easier if you just work out your relationship rather than giving up and quitting." To which Tino adds that "nothing comes easy. If you really want to make it work, you have to work at it."[2]

The Influence of Friends

Tino and Donna persisted, but with many teen parents the breaking down of their relationship occurs at a much earlier point in time. In many cases that point comes when the many pressures of teen parenting are heightened by a third-party interaction. It is then that issues of undue influence and jealousy arise.

This may not initially involve a romantic entanglement with another person on the part of the teen father or teen mother. That may occur later, but the initial third-party issues are more likely to have to do with family and friends. The feelings involved are more likely to be related to power than romantic attachment.

A common source of friction is the friends of the teen father, and the teen mother's perception of their influence on him. That perception may be skewed or exaggerated or it may be true. Either way, the teen father must deal with his co-parent's convictions that his friends are affecting his behavior in ways that result in his neglecting her and their child. He is embarrassed to change diapers and perform other household tasks in front of them. He goes out with them too often and stays out too late. He gets drunk or high with them. In front of them he becomes macho and surly with her and their child to prove he isn't henpecked. He cares more about their opinion than he does about hers, would rather be with them than with his child. They say things about her behind her back and he lets them. They are pulling him farther and farther away.

The teen father accuses his co-parent of being jealous of his friends. He's right. She is jealous. But they are his friends and he doesn't want to lose them. On the other hand, he doesn't want to heighten the tension with the teen mother to the breaking point and risk harming his relationship with his child. There is no easy answer. He and his child's mother can try talking it out, reaching a compromise—so much time with mother and child, so much time with friends—but, in truth, such stopgap measures don't usually last too long. One better solution, perhaps, is to face up to the situation squarely and make arrangements for a future where separation from his child's mother allows for frequent and regular contact with his child.

Dealing with the New Man

When teen parents split up and the young mother takes up with another man, the problems for the teen father go well beyond sexual jealousy. Sometimes the new man is older and able to provide financially for the mother and child in the way that the young father can't. He may be her ticket to escaping from her parents' house. He may become possessive and not want the father of his woman's child hanging around. Even if that isn't an up-front problem, the new man's presence may interfere with scheduling father-child visits.

The teen dad may feel that his father role is being undermined by the new man. He may resent the new male taking over his authority with the child. He may feel pushed out. Realistically, there will be some jealousy, and jealousy often gets in the way of establishing the compromises necessary to create a smooth and ongoing father-child relationship.

It is possible to work out such compromises, but it may take time. Where there are bad feelings, teen parents "may diminish the amount of contact as a way to avoid conflict." However, the study in *Families in Society* notes that "although mothers may report no contact with the father of the child at any one point in time, they may have contact with the father at some later juncture." Tempers cool and where there is love for a child, resentments are set aside and regular visits may resume.[8]

Over the short term, though, it can be very stormy. When Gerard, who became a father at eighteen, split with his child Eric's mother to live with another woman, she got out an order of protection against him that made it impossible for him to see his son. This was followed up by police showing up on Gerard's birthday with a warrant for his arrest. The charges were dismissed, and then Gerard hired a lawyer. "I fought for visiting rights and I got it," he says. "The judge said, 'He's entitled to see his son two, three days a week whether you like it or not!'"

With the passage of time, both Gerard and Eric's mother, Teresa, have cooled down considerably and learned to work together to behave in the child's best interest. "Now that we're not together, we can communicate," Gerard reports. His new girlfriend is pregnant and Teresa is pregnant by another man. Nevertheless, Gerard sees Eric regularly during the week and often takes him for weekends. Gerard and Teresa continue to work it out and, says Gerard, "We're the best of friends."[9]

Multiple Relationships

Maintaining ongoing relationships with children can be particularly difficult for those teen fathers who have had more than one child with more than one young woman. In the sexually active teen world, such situations are more common than is generally recognized. The teen father finds himself torn between obligations to two mothers and two children, sometimes even more than that. Time and money spent on one mother and child will inevitably be resented by the other. The teen father is in the position of older men with two families, but without their resources.

He may have a legal obligation to both mothers and both children. Studies indicate that most teen fathers want to meet such obligations, but in situations where more than one mother-child is involved, they simply are not able to do so. It's pointless to assign blame. The teen father is trapped, and he needs help. In such cases psychological counseling is recommended, and as we shall see in the next chapter, such help may be available without charge from a variety of organizations.

Financial obligations aside, the teen father must come up with a juggling act if he wishes to see his children on an ongoing basis. It takes an effort to maintain contact with two families and either go to school, or hold down a job when one is still not fully an adult. The impressive thing is that many young fathers—even those who may fall short—make the effort to sustain a relationship with more than one child.

Seduced and Abandoned?

Even more impressive are those teen fathers who insist on their paternity in the face of partners who want nothing from them, and want them to have nothing to do with their children.

These are the minority of adolescent men who become involved with older women. Sometimes fearful of charges of seduction, or even sexual abuse for having had sex with a minor, after childbirth such women frequently try to exclude the young partner from their lives. This means excluding the teen males from the lives of their children as well.

The teen father is relieved of all responsibility, but at the same time with no contact—without sharing child care—he has little chance of bonding with his offspring. Many of these young men find the burden of having a child they can't see too heavy to bear easily. Should the woman become involved with a man her own age, or perhaps even marry, the teen dad may find himself completely excluded from his child's life.

Legal recourse is available to the teen father in this position. Court decisions have recently swung in favor of granting paternity rights regardless of the youth of the father. He can choose DNA testing as a means of proving his paternity. As with psychological help, legal aid is available to him from a variety of sources described in the following chapter.

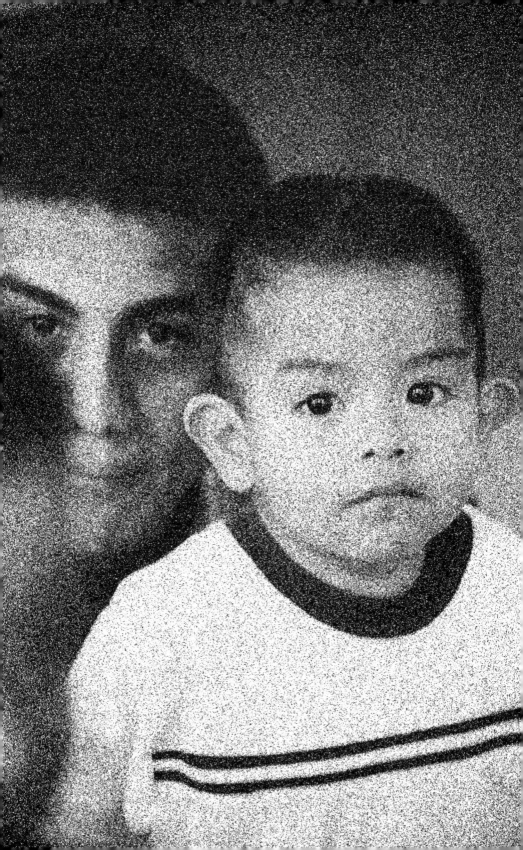

9.
HELP IS AVAILABLE

The problems that plague so many teenagers today, including pregnancy, cannot be overcome unless we find ways to give these young people a belief in themselves and their futures. . . . These include an adequate education, access to a good job, and the means to attain economic self-sufficiency. Providing these opportunities requires a wide range of strategies: strengthening our educational system, restoring communities that have become hazardous to the well-being of children and families, making early childhood development programs available, and working to combat the multiple problems associated with child poverty.[1]
                    —A Report from the Children's Defense
                    Fund, *The State of America's Children,* 1998

For many of the reasons mentioned in the previous chapters, the teen father often feels isolated. Paternity weighs heavily on him, and he doesn't know where to turn for help. Much of this burden, however, is because of his own ignorance of the many organizations that offer assistance to teen fathers in a variety of areas including life skills, career and job counseling, legal aid, educational alternatives, child rearing, and others.

Federal Aid Programs

Some of this aid will come from the government and will be subject to certain rules and restrictions. It may be set up on a state, regional, or community basis. All of it must conform with the 1996 federal Personal Responsibility and Work Opportunity Reconciliation Act described in Chapter Four. One part of this act which can apply directly to teen fathers is the Work Opportunity and Welfare-to-Work Tax Credits provision, which was renewed on December 17, 1999, to run through December 31, 2001.

The U.S. Department of Labor defines the Work Opportunity Tax Credit (WOTC) as "a federal income tax credit that encourages employers to hire eight targeted groups of job seekers." Teen fathers are often members of one or another of these groups. They may have been members of families on welfare, or the mothers of their children may be receiving help from TANF or food stamps. They may have directly or indirectly received Supplemental Security Income benefits. They may be eligible for employment in Empowerment Zones or Enterprise Communities programs through which WOTC "can reduce employer federal tax liability by as much as $2,400 per new hire." WOTC is one of many government programs "designed to help job seekers most in need of employment gain on-the-job experience and move toward economic self-sufficiency."[2]

A sister program is the Welfare-to-Work Tax Credit, which "can reduce employer federal tax liability by as much as $8,500 per new hire." In 1999, 104,998 applicants were hired by Welfare-to-Work programs. That same year 335,707 people found jobs with WOTC programs.

These programs are located around the country in what the Labor Department defines as federal Empowerment Zones (EZ's) and Enterprise Communities (EC's). The teen father can find the one nearest him by calling the local America's Job Bank office or the nearest U.S. Department of Labor Bureau of Apprenticeship and Training Office. If there is no EZ/EC program in his area, he may be referred to a local equivalent such as the Newark, New Jersey, Enterprise Community which is run by the state with both federal and state money. There are many other local programs augmenting the federal EZ/EC effort. Most of them, as well as many of the EZ/EC programs, also hire sixteen- and seventeen-year-olds as Summer Youth Employees.

Being hired as an EZ/EC employee has made a difference for Cesar who became a new father shortly after his seventeenth birthday. "It's like a foothold," he says. "Sure it's only a temporary job, but I talk to other guys in the program and to some of the people over me, and I'm learning about other government programs I can be eligible for. I won't have to go back to shaping up every day to unload trucks. I can get training along with a job." He grins. "Even Anita's father doesn't think I'm such a bum anymore and I get to see her and Raoul—that's our baby—pretty often."[3]

"Devoted Dads"

"Devoted Dads," one of the more innovative EZ/EC programs, was started in Tacoma, Washington, in December 1997. It is a public/private partnership to help young, noncustodial fathers in the financial and emotional support of their offspring. "Devoted Dads is a very exciting and important model for the nation to help fathers contribute to the healthy growth of their children," according to former Secretary of the U.S. Department of Health and Human Services Donna E. Shalala.[4]

Secretary Shalala approved a child support waiver for teen fathers enrolled in the Tacoma Enterprise Community. It was the first such waiver granted to an EZ/EC program. The waiver allowed the state of Washington to use federal funds normally used only for child support enforcement activities to support the project. The idea was totake the pressure off these fathers temporarily while they received the help and guidance necessary to become self-sufficient and to become active parents.

To reach this goal, Devoted Dads provides a mix of public education and services designed to help young fathers. These include a self-help and mediation program to resolve conflicts, peer education on paternity by young unwed fathers, programs on teen parenting for young fathers, and counseling. A major thrust of the program, said Secretary Shalala, is "to ensure that fathers provide child support to their children as families move from welfare to self-sufficiency." After four years (in December 2001), this Welfare-to-Work program will be reevaluated to see how well it has met its goals.[5]

Apprenticeship and Job Corps

A spin-off of the Welfare-to-Work Tax Credit program is the Welfare-to-Work Coalition to Sustain Success set up by former Vice President Al Gore. It consists of a coalition of civic groups, which tailor their services to meet the needs of those they are helping. They particularly target young people, including teen fathers. Among the charter members of the coalition are the Boys and Girls Clubs of America, the Baptist Joint Committee, the United Way, and the YMCA. A good starting point for teen fathers seeking aid would be any one of these groups.

Another offshoot is the Welfare-to-Work Partnership chaired by United Airlines CEO Gerald Greenwald. Its purpose is to move those receiving public assistance into jobs in the private sector. It is presently focusing on youth in twelve cities with high levels of poverty.

One federal program that may be of particular interest to teen fathers because of its long-term goals is the Individuals Apprenticeship project run by the Employment and Training Administration (ETA) of the U.S. Department of Labor. It combines on-the-job training with related classroom instruction to teach both practical and theoretical aspects of highly skilled occupations. These programs are sponsored by employer and labor groups in twenty-seven states. Applicants must be over sixteen years old and must demonstrate the ability, aptitude, and basic education needed to master the occupation they have chosen. Applications may be obtained from the local Bureau of Apprenticeship and Training (BAT) Regional Office, or from BAT in Washington, D.C.

The largest federal program aimed at young people is Job Corps with 111 centers in 46 states. Since its inception in 1964,

"Job Corps has guided more than 1.5 million young people away from lives filled with poverty, unemployment, crime and welfare and steered them toward brighter futures filled with self-confidence, independence, and productive employment." Job Corps "is a full-time, year-round residential program that offers a comprehensive array of training, education, and supportive services, including supervised dormitory housing, meals, medical care, and counseling." This includes counseling and other support services appropriate for teen fathers.[6]

The MALE Pilot Program

Government aid programs are usually structured to help a large and diverse population with a variety of needs, and don't specifically address the problems of teen fathers. They tend to be more focused on employment goals, and less on the psychological and sociological pressures affecting adolescent dads. However, a pilot program of the Educational Resources Information Center (ERIC) of the U.S. Department of Education was set up to deal specifically with these issues.

Called Maximizing a Life Experience (MALE), the program focused narrowly on eight adolescent fathers. Its goals were "to help the young men understand their emotional rights (to express feelings and concerns and receive emotional support) and responsibilities, as well as their legal rights and responsibilities, and to learn about available resources." Specifically, this meant putting them in touch with their feelings as teen fathers, helping them deal with their present situation, obtaining factual information about contraception and pregnancy, identifying and exploring their present and future options, training them to deal with problems and make sound decisions, introducing the resources available to them and showing them how to use them.[7]

Experts in psychology and conflict resolution, and representatives from Planned Parenthood and the Legal Aid Society, dealt with specific problems of the teen father participants. Indeed, learning the legal rights of unwed teenage fathers was the main reason some teen dads joined the group. An attorney from the Legal Aid Society was provided with a copy of the group's questions and responded to them as well as to additional questions.

In a follow-up of MALE's eight group members a year after the program ended, "four were in college or technical school, two were in the military, and two were still in high school. None were married or had a second child, and all were continuing to contribute toward the support of their first child. The only change in the follow-up two years later was that one young man had dropped out of college, and one had graduated from high school. Both of them were working full time."[8]

Parents as Teachers (PAT)

MALE pointed a direction for many larger programs by state and local governments and private organizations, which directly address the concerns of teen dads. One of the most extensive is the Parents as Teachers (PAT) campaign, which covers forty-nine states and six countries. Run by the Parents as Teachers National Center, Inc., in St. Louis, Missouri, PAT believes that teen fathers are not given enough attention although studies strongly indicate that they play a critical role in determining how their children develop.

The PAT Institute offers training for professionals who work with teen parents of children from birth through age three. The focus is on adolescent development, recruitment and retention of teen mothers and fathers, family dynamics, multi-generational issues, and much more. A 225-page guide includes organizational resources and written materials designed to meet the needs of teen parents and of the programs that serve them.

Those trained by PAT either return to their communities and start programs, many of them directed at teen fathers and mothers, or incorporate PAT principles into ongoing programs, some of which specifically target teen fathers. These programs can help teen parents make use of other local resources and service providers such as infant diagnostic services, speech and hearing clinics, programs for children with special needs, health and mental health agencies, social-service agencies, learning resources for children and teen parents, and others.

Independent evaluations of PAT programs have found that the teen parents served are more confident in their parenting skills and knowledge and read more to their child, that their children have significantly improved language, problem solving skills, and social development between birth and age three, that these gains carry over to the early elementary grades and result in higher scores on standardized reading and math tests, and that the teen parents in PAT programs tend to stay involved in their child's education, both at school and at home.

Coast-to-Coast Programs

Of the many programs across the nation offering services to teen fathers, those which are not staffed by PAT-trained volunteers are nevertheless influenced by PAT's approach. One of the most successful of these is the Insights Teen Parent Program run by the Volunteer Center in Portland, Oregon. The program pairs off teen fathers with mentors—adults who provide knowledgeable support in such areas as career focusing, building independence, management of time and stress, housing assistance, and crisis intervention. It also provides parenting classes which teach child-care techniques, as well as providing diapers, baby formula, and other supplies as needed.

Another city of Portland, this one across the country in Maine, operates a program called Teen Parenting Services (TPS). It is structured around the mixed messages that teen fathers get from society. "They are blamed for impregnating a girl and leaving, yet families are penalized (by welfare rules, for example) for having males around," points out the program director. "And young fathers aren't offered the opportunity to learn how to be a dad and a partner."[9] To correct this, TPS teams young fathers up with their baby's mother to actively share parental responsibilities. It encourages the teen father to stay with the family as much as is practical and to commit himself to being a parent. TPS's primary aim is a two-parent family; its alternative aim is for the teen father to maintain a relationship with his child even when he and the mother are not together.

In Arizona, the STEP-UP program with mentoring for young fathers aged sixteen to twenty-two is a continuation by the city of Phoenix, backed up by local corporate sponsors, of a federal project that ran from September 1992 through February 1995. STEP-UP has developed a highly effective "one-step-at-a-time" program that first deals with the young father's immediate problems, works to stabilize his situation, and then helps him to identify and capitalize on available resources, which can lead to real growth and development. It is a multidimensional program offering a wide variety of counseling and support activities designed to conform to the particular need of the individual teen father. One innovation—the Family Training Camp—has proven particularly successful with young fathers who were gang members, establishing a turf-neutral environment where rivals can find common ground in discussions of the problems of teen paternity. The Phoenix STEP-UP program has attracted statewide and national attention, and several other cities in Arizona and elsewhere have set up similar programs.

"Family Training Camp has maybe turned me around," says African-American teen father and gang member Jason of Tucson, Arizona. "There were Indians and Mexicans and whites there—guys we used to go against. We'd talk about how we felt being young and not enough cash and changing diapers—stuff like that. We talked about our gangs too, hanging tight, and all the bad stuff and where it could lead, like jail, or worse. Cutting loose from the gang, that's hard. I'm gonna try, though. I mean, I don't feel the hate anymore. I'm like more into my kid."[10]

Local and Regional Projects

Following are some of the many other programs across the country offering help and services to teen fathers:

California: the Developing Adolescent Dads for Success (DADS) in Santa Monica; AltaMed Youth Services of Commerce; Teen Family Service of West Covina.

Connecticut: the Teen Fathers Program in the Bridgeport/Stratford area.

Indiana: Booker T. Washington Alternative School in Terre Haute.

Kentucky: Jefferson County Public Schools' Teen Parent Program.

Maryland: the Healthy Start Program in Baltimore.

Minnesota: the Dads Make a Difference initiative in Ramsey County.

Missouri: the Parenting and Paternity Alliance (PAPA).

New Mexico: New Futures School of Albuquerque.

New York City: The Door; the Fatherhood Project; the Youth Research Institute; the Adolescent Medical Department of

Source Notes

CHAPTER ONE

1. Author's interviews, New York City, November 3, 1999, and January 20, 2000.
2. Marc Lacey, "Teenage Birthrate in U.S. Falls Again," *The New York Times,* October 27, 1999, p. A16.
3. Nancy C. Larson, Jon M. Hussey, Mary Rogers Gilmore, and Lewayne D. Gilchrist, "What about dad? Fathers of children born to school-age mothers," *Families in Society,* May 1996, p. 279.
4. No byline, "Woman Forbidden from Seeing Teen Father of Her Child," *The Los Angeles Times,* April 29, 1999, p. 4.
5. Author's interview, New York City, November 1, 1999.
6. Paul Lang and Susan S. Lang, *Teen Fathers* (New York: Franklin Watts, 1995), p. 24.
7. Lacey, *The New York Times,* p. A16.
8. Author's Interview, Hewlett, NY, October 23, 1999.
9. Lacey, *The New York Times,* p. A16.
10. Ibid.
11. Anu Rangarajan, and Philip Gleason, "Young unwed fathers of AFDC children: Do they provide support?" *Demography; Population Association of America,* May 1998, pp. 175–186.
12. William D. Allen, and William J. Doherty, "The responsibilities of fatherhood as perceived by African-American teenage fathers," *Families in Society: The Journal of Contemporary Human Services,* March 1996, pp. 142–155.

CHAPTER TWO

1. Janet Bode, *Kids Still Having Kids: Talking About Teen Pregnancy* (Danbury, CT: Franklin Watts, 1999), p. 38.
2. Ibid, p. 61.
3. William D. Allen, and William J. Doherty, "The responsibilities of fatherhood as perceived by African-American teenage fathers," *Families in Society: The Journal of Contemporary Human Services,* March 1996, pp. 142–155.
4. Author's interviews, New York City, November 3, 1999 and January 20, 2000.
5. Wayne C. Huey, "Counseling Teenage Fathers: The 'Maximizing a Life Experience'" (MALE) Group, ERIC Digest. Internet: http://165.224.67/databases/ERIC_digests/ed341891.html
6. Paul Lang, and Susan S. Lang, *Teen Fathers* (New York: Franklin Watts, 1995), p. 45.
7. Huey, Internet: http://165.224.67/databases/ERIC_digests/ed341891.html

CHAPTER THREE

1. William D. Allen, and William J. Doherty, "The responsibilities of fatherhood as perceived by African-American teenage fathers," *Families in Society: The Journal of Contemporary Human Services,* March 1996, pp. 142–155.
2. Ben Westhoff, "Teen Fathers Need Support Too, Says Director of Center," *St. Louis Post Dispatch*, October 9, 1997, p. A 15. Internet:http://proquest.umi.com/pqdweb?TS=...&Sid=1&Idx=28&Deli=1&RQT=309&Dtp=1
3. Allen and Doherty, pp. 142–155.
4. Author's interview, New York City, November 10, 1999.
5. Jeanne Warren Lindsay, MA, CFCS, *Teenage Couples: Coping with Reality* (Buena Park, CA: Morning Glory Press, 1995), p. 84.
6. Author's interview, New York City, November 10, 1999.
7. Ibid.
8. Thomas Maier, *Dr. Spock: An American Life* (New York: Harcourt Brace & Company, 1998), p. 206.
9. Dr. Penelope Leach, *Your Baby & Child: From Birth to Age Five* (New York: Alfred A. Knopf, 1990), p. 43.
10. Maier, p. 207.
11. Alfred T. Lane, M.D., *Bathing Basics,* Internet: http://www.pampers.com/primer/2353
12. Dr. Kathleen Alfano, Ph.D., "Play Tips," Internet: http://www.pampers.com/activity/newpt.jhtml

13. Glenn P. Matney, M.D., *Flush With SUCCESS,* Internet: http://babyparenting.miningco.com/home/babyparenting/gi/dy namic/offsite.htm?site=http://victorvalley.com/health%26law/hl aw%2Dfeb/matney.htm
14. Mira Gohel, James J. Diamond, and Christopher V. Chambers, "Attitudes towards sexual responsibility and parenting: An exploratory study of young urban males," (New York: *Family Planning Perspectives,* November/December 1997), Document 4.
15. Allen and Doherty, pp. 142–155.

CHAPTER FOUR
1. Margi Trapani, *Reality Check: Teenage Fathers Speak Out* (New York: The Rosen Publishing Group, Inc., 1997), p. 29.
2. A Report from the Children's Defense Fund, *The State of America's Children* (Boston: Beacon Press, 1998), p. 88.
3. Author's interview, New York City, November 1, 1999.
4. William Marsiglio, "Young nonresident biological fathers," *Marriage & Family Review,* 1995, p.325. Internet: http://www.haworthpressinc.com/
5. Nancy C. Larson, Jon M. Hussey, Mary Rogers Gillmore, and Lewayne D. Gilchrist, "What about dad? Fathers of children born to school-age mothers," *Families in Society,* May 1996, Document Five.
6. Marsiglio, p.325.
7. Author's interview, Hewlett, NY, October 23, 1999.

CHAPTER FIVE
1. Janet Bode, *Kids Still Having Kids: Talking About Teen Pregnancy* (Danbury, CT: Franklin Watts, 1999), p.127.
2. Jeanne Warren Lindsay, MA, CFCS, *Teenage Couples: Coping with Reality* (Buena Park, CA: Morning Glory Press, 1995), p.78.
3. Ibid.
4. William Marsiglio, "Adolescent Fathers in the United States: Their Initial Living Arrangements, Marital Experience and Educational Outcomes," *Family Planning Perspectives,* November/December 1987, p. 240.
5. Steven L. Nock, "The consequences of premarital fatherhood," *American Sociological Review,* April 1998, pp. 250–263.
6. Margi Trapani, *Reality Check: Teenage Fathers Speak Out* (New York: The Rosen Publishing Group, Inc., 1997), p. 29.

7. William D. Allen, and William J. Doherty, "The responsibilities of fatherhood as perceived by African-American teenage fathers," *Families in Society: The Journal of Contemporary Human Services,* March 1996, pp. 142–155.) A study by *Family Planning Perspectives.*
8. Ibid.
9. Ibid.
10. Ibid.
11. Ibid.
12. April Kaplan, "Father-Child relationships in Welfare Reform," *Welfare Information Network Issue Notes,* Vol. 2, No. 3, January 1998.
13. Allen and Doherty, *Families in Society: The Journal of Contemporary Human Services,* pp. 142–155.
14. Ibid.

CHAPTER SIX
1. Karen Gravelle, and Leslie Petersen, *Teenage Fathers* (New York: Julian Messner, 1992), pp. 6–7.
2. A Report from the Children's Defense Fund, *The State of America's Children* (Boston: Beacon Press, 1998), p. 95.
3. Author's interview, New York City, December 15, 1999.
4. Ibid.
5. Ibid.
6. Paul Lang, and Susan S. Lang, *Teen Fathers* (New York: Franklin Watts, 1995), p. 73.
7. M. Gohel, J. J. Diamond, and C. V. Chambers, "Attitudes towards sexual responsibility and parenting: an exploratory study of young urban males," *Family Planning Perspectives,* Vol. 29, No. 6, November/December 1997. From The Alan Guttmacher Institute, Internet: www.agi-usa.org/sex_behave/
8. Ibid.
9. Lang and Lang, p. 73.
10. William Marsiglio, "Young nonresident biological fathers," *Marriage & Family Review,* 1995, p.325.
11. Lang and Lang, p. 73.
12. Margi Trapani, *Reality Check: Teenage Fathers Speak Out* (New York: The Rosen Publishing Group, Inc., 1997), p. 15.
13. *Family Planning Perspectives,* Vol. 29, No. 6, November/December 1997. From The Alan Guttmacher Institute, Internet: www.agi-usa.org

14. April Kaplan, "Father-Child Relationships in Welfare Reform," *Welfare Information Network,* Vol. 2, No. 3, January 1998.
15. Earl Ofari Hutchinson, Ph.D., "Criminalizing a Generation," Internet:http://www.afrocentricnews.net/html/ofari_criminal.html
16. Internet: http://turnpike.net/~jnr/inprison.htm
17. Kaplan, op. cit.

CHAPTER SEVEN
1. Margi Trapani, *Reality Check: Teenage Fathers Speak Out* (New York: The Rosen Publishing Group, Inc., 1997), p. 21.
2. Author's interviews, January 14, 2000 (phone), and January 20, 2000 (in person).
3. Ibid.
4. Ibid.
5. Ibid.
6. Jeanne Warren Lindsay, MA, CFCS, *Teenage Couples: Expectations and Reality* (Buena Park, CA: Morning Glory Press, 1996), p.58.
7. Ibid, p. 61.
8. Ibid, p. 60.
9. Author's interview, Hewlett, NY, October 23, 1999.
10. Paul Lang, and Susan S. Lang, *Teen Fathers* (New York: Franklin Watts, 1995), p. 45.
11. Author's interview, Hewlett, NY, October 23, 1999.

CHAPTER EIGHT
1. Jeanne Warren Lindsay, MA, CFCS, *Teenage Couples: Expectations and Reality* (Buena Park, CA: Morning Glory Press, 1996), p.52.
2. Jeanne Warren Lindsay, MA, CFCS, *Teenage Couples: Coping with Reality* (Buena Park, CA: Morning Glory Press, 1995), pp. 166–167.
3. Lindsay, *Teenage Couples: Expectations and Reality*, p.78.
4. Ibid, p. 79.
5. Author's interviews, January 14, 2000 (phone), and January 20, 2000 (in person).
6. Janet Bode, *Kids Still Having Kids: Talking About Teen Pregnancy* (Danbury, CT: Franklin Watts, 1999), pp. 129–130.
7. Nancy C. Larson, Jon M. Hussey, Mary Rogers Gillmore, and Lewayne D. Gilchrist, "What about dad? Fathers of children

born to school-age mothers," *Families in Society: The Journal of Contemporary Human Services,* May 1996, p. 279.

8. Ibid.

9. Karen Gravelle, and Leslie Petersen, *Teenage Fathers* (New York: Julian Messner, 1992), p. 79.

CHAPTER NINE

1. A Report from the Children's Defense Fund, *The State of America's Children* (Boston: Beacon Press, 1998), pp. 100–101.

2. "Work Opportunity and Welfare-to-Work Tax Credits," November 1998, U.S. Department of Labor. Internet: http://www.doleta.gov/employer/wotc.htm

3. Author's interviews, November 3, 1999, and January 29, 2000.

4. Michael Kharfen, "HHS Approves Child Support Waiver for 'Devoted Dads' Project in Tacoma, Washington, Enterprise Community," U.S. Department of Health and Human Services Press Release, December 18, 1997. Internet:http://www. os.dhhs.gov/news/press/1997pres/971218b.html

5. Ibid.

6. "What Is Job Corps?," ETA Individuals Job Corps. Internet: Http://www.doleta.gov/individ/jobcorps.htm

7. Wayne C. Huey, "Counseling Teenage Fathers: The 'Maximizing a Life Experience' (MALE) Group." *ERIC Digest,* ERIC Clearinghouse on Counseling and Personnel Services, Ann Arbor, MI., Internet: http://www.ed.gov/databases/ERIC_Digests/ed341891.html

8. Ibid.

9. CDF Reports, November 1998 Bulletin. Internet:http://www.ncpta.org/Bulletin/NOV98/nov98motherandfather.html

10. Author's interview, January 21, 2000.

Organizations to Contact

Adolescent Medical Department, Montefiore Hospital, 111 East 210th Street, Bronx, NY
Phone: (718) 920-4321

Alan Guttmacher Institute, 120 Wall Street, New York, NY 10005
Phone: (212) 248-1111

AltaMed Youth Services, 2476 South Atlantic Boulevard, Commerce, CA 90040
Phone: (213) 980-3061; Fax: (213) 980-3067

Bureau of Apprenticeship and Training of the Employment and Training Administration (ETA) U.S. Department of Labor, 200 Constitution Avenue NW, Washington, DC
Phone: (202) 219-5921

Educational Resources Information Center (ERIC) of the U.S. Department of Education
Fatherhood Project, 330 Seventh Avenue, New York, NY
Phone: (212) 465-2044

Institute for Responsible Fatherhood and Family Revitalization, 1146 19th Street NW, Suite 800, Washington, DC 20036

Latin American Youth Center, 1419 Columbia Road NW, Washington, DC 20009
Phone: (202) 319-2225

Legal Aid Society, 90 Church Street, New York, NY, 10007
Phone (212) 577-3300

MELD for Young Dads, 123 B. 3rd Street, Suite 507, Minneapolis,
MN 55401

National Center on Fathers and Families, Graduate School of
Education, University of Pennsylvania, 3700 Walnut St., Box 58,
Philadelphia, PA 19104

Parents as Teachers National Center, Inc., 10176 Corporate Square
Drive, Suite 230, St. Louis, MO 63132
Phone: (314) 432-4330; Fax: (314) 432-8963

Planned Parenthood Federation of America, Inc., 810 Seventh
Avenue, New York, NY 10019
Phone: (212) 541-7800

Planned Parenthood of New York City, Inc., Margaret Sanger
Square, 26 Bleecker Street, New York, NY 10012-2413
Phone: (212) 274-7200

Teen Family Service, 1720 W. Cameron Ave., Suite 100, West
Covina, CA 91791
Phone: (626) 338-9200; Fax: (626) 856-1560

Teen Fathers Program, YMCA of Greater Bridgeport, 651 State
Street, Bridgeport, CT 06604
Phone: (203) 334-5551

The Door: A Center of Alternatives, 121 Avenue of the Americas,
New York, NY 10013
Phone: (212) 274-1913 or 941-9090

Trinity House Problem Adolescent Program, St. Luke-Roosevelt
Hospital, 1111 Amsterdam Avenue, New York, NY 10025
Phone: (212) 523-4000.

Welfare to Work Partnership
Phone (toll-free): 1-888-USAJOB1

Work Opportunity Tax Credits & Welfare to Work Tax Credits
Phone (toll-free) 1-877-828-2050 for state contact information.

Youth Research Institute, 40 E. 55th Street, New York, NY
Phone: (212) 752-3489

Internet Sites

Alan Guttmacher Institute:
www.agi-usa.org/

America's Job Bank:
http://www.ajb.dni.us/seeker/search/

Educational Resources Information Center (ERIC):
www.accesseric.org

Education Resource Organization Directory (EROD):
http://www.ed.gov/

Franciscan at St. John—Young Fathers:
http://www.franciscan-stjohn.com/youngfathers.html

Insights Teen Parent Program:
http://portland.citysearch.com/E/V/PDXOR/0003/98/76/cs1.html

Job Corps:
http://www.doleta.gov/individ/jobcorps.htm

Latin American Youth Center:
http://www.charitablechoices.org/LatinAmericanYouthCenter/

Pampers Parenting Institute:
http://www.pampers.com/

Parents as Teachers National Center:
http://www.patnc.org/teenparn.htm

The Fatherhood Project:
http://sophia.smith.edu/~sgirard/fhp.html

U.S. Department of Education:
http://www.ed.gov/

Welfare to Work Partnership:
www.welfaretowork.org

Work Opportunity Tax Credits and Welfare to Work Tax Credits:
http://www.doleta.gov/employer/wotc.htm

Further Reading

Ayer, Eleanor H. *Everything You Need to Know About Teen Fatherhood*, rev. ed. New York: The Rosen Publishing Group, 1995.

Bode, Janet. *Kids Still Having Kids,* rev. ed. Danbury, CT: Franklin Watts, 1999.

Gravelle, Karen, and Leslie Petersen. *Teenage Fathers.* New York: Julian Messner, 1992.

Hutchinson, Earl Ofari. *Black Fatherhood: The Guide to Male Parenting.* Los Angeles: Middle Passage, 1995.

Lang, Paul, and Susan S. Lang. *Teen Fathers.* New York: Franklin Watts, 1995.

Lindsay, Jeanne Warren. *Teenage Couples: Expectations and Reality.* Buena Park, CA: Morning Glory Press, 1996.

Trapani, Margi. *Reality Check: Teenage Fathers Speak Out.* New York: The Rosen Publishing Group, Inc., 1997.

Index